TOWARDS A DUAL INCOME TAX?

Scandinavian and Austrian Experiences

by

LEIF MUTÉN

PETER B. SØRENSEN AND KÅRE P. HAGEN

and

BERND GENSER

Foundation for European Fiscal Studies
Erasmus University Rotterdam

KLUWER LAW INTERNATIONAL
LONDON – THE HAGUE – BOSTON

Published by Kluwer Law International
Sterling House
66 Wilton Road
London SW1V 1DE
United Kingdom

Kluwer Law International incorporates
the publishing programmes of
Graham & Trotman Ltd,
Kluwer Law & Taxation Publishers
and Martinus Nijhoff Publishers.

Sold and distributed in the USA and Canada
by Kluwer Law International
675 Massachusetts Avenue
Cambridge MA 02139
USA

In all other countries, sold and distributed
by Kluwer Law International
P.O. Box 85889
2508 CN The Hague
The Netherlands

ISBN 90-411-0928-5

First published 1996

British Library Cataloguing in Publication Data and Library of Congress Cataloging-in-Publication Data is available

CONTENTS

PREFACE

In recent years, the Scandinavian countries and Finland have implemented far-reaching reforms of their individual and company income taxes. These countries have replaced their so-called global income taxes by dual income taxes under which the tax treatment of capital income is separated from the tax treatment of labor income. Labor income continues to be taxed at (high) progressive rates, but capital income is taxed at a low, uniform rate. Austria also has moved towards a dual income tax by introducing, among other things, a flat, final source withholding tax on interest.

The dual income taxes were adopted primarily to counter the growing erosion of the capital income tax base. As elsewhere, capital mobility and financial innovation had greatly increased opportunities for domestic and cross-border tax arbitrage. Consequently, capital income was taxed lightly or, more likely, not at all – and in any case at widely differing rates. These countries realized that capital mobility precluded the imposition of high tax rates on capital income, whilst tax arbitrage nullified the workings of a progressive rate structure. Hence, they concluded that capital income should be taxed at a low, uniform rate. Interestingly, as a result, revenue from capital income taxation increased.

The dual income tax is an interesting innovation that deserves wider discussion and perhaps imitation. Therefore, on May 19, 1995, the Foundation for European Fiscal Studies of Erasmus University Rotterdam organized a symposium to review various aspects of the dual income tax. This brochure contains the papers presented at the symposium. The first paper, by Leif Mutén, examines the reasons for Sweden's move towards the dual income tax, noting the difficulties of separating capital and labor income accruing in proprietorships and closed companies. Kåre Hagen and Peter Sørensen, in the second paper, dwell at length on this issue, which has been called the Achilles heel of the dual income tax. In the last paper, Bernd Genser surveys and evaluates the Austrian income tax reform.

The Foundation for Fiscal Studies is grateful to its foreign guests for submitting their papers for publication in the EFS series. Thanks are also due Ruud Okker of the Dutch Central Planning Bureau and Leo Stevens of Erasmus University for their contributions to the discussion at the seminar. Marja Sjerp was most helpful in organizing the seminar and handling the administrative arrangements. Once again, Jeanne Bovenberg's expertise was indispensable in preparing the brochure for publication.

Sijbren Cnossen
Editor

DUAL INCOME TAXATION: SWEDISH EXPERIENCE

LEIF MUTÉN

Stockholm School of Economics

I. INTRODUCTION

Once upon a time, the state of the art of taxation prescribed a synthetic or global income tax, rather than a schedular tax imposed separately on each type of income. The traditional schedular tax systems, particularly in countries sharing the Latin tradition, were frowned upon, and the principle was firmly adhered to that only a global income tax could fulfill the requirement of correctly adapting the tax burden to the ability to pay.[1]

Another principle, also regarded as intrinsic to the concept of taxation in accordance with ability to pay, called for a heavier tax on unearned income than on earned income. This principle could be implemented by rate differentiation, best well known from the UK, or by the imposition of a separate net wealth tax. The same goal, of course, could be achieved on the cost side, by generous standard deductions offered to people with employment income. As to the definition of what constitutes earned and unearned income, respectively, the problem has been particularly acute with respect to business people, whose profits could be seen partly as earned income, since they worked

1. For a systematic treatment of this issue, see Plasschaert, S., Schedular, Global and Dualistic Patterns of Income Taxation, *IBFD*, Amsterdam, 1988.

in the business, and partly as yield on the capital they had invested in the business.

Meanwhile, rate differentiation has taken on another meaning in many countries. The dual income tax system recently introduced in Finland, Norway, and Sweden is an illustrative case.[2] In all three countries, the old ideal of a global income tax embracing income from all kinds of sources, with current losses of one income source being deductible from the sum of positive income from other sources, has been abandoned. Moreover, concurrent with a general reduction of the highest progressive tax rates, the nominal rate of tax on income from capital has been reduced even more.

This development was certainly not generally anticipated. One might rather see it as surprising, particularly in view of the important role played by income taxation in these countries, and the high progressive rates normally applied by them. Nevertheless, it is perhaps just because the rates used to be so high, that the weaknesses of the global income tax came to the fore and gave rise to a fundamental reform.

The first steps along the road of this new development were taken in the form of ceiling provisions with respect to deductions for net interest paid on non-business debt. It was found that as long as there was no general distinction between interest on consumer credit and other interest payments, notably mortgage interest, the tax base with respect to income from capital was de facto negative.[3]

Taxpayers saw to it that the positive yield on their investments took non-taxable or tax-privileged forms. This could be done by investing in homes (the imputed rental value not being taxable) or in other real property treated similarly for tax purposes, or even pieces of art, antiques, and the like, that promised capital gains rather than a periodic yield. Other investments offering the same tax benefits included insurance savings, particularly those following the familiar pattern for pensions, with little or no tax on the current yield of the

2. With the tax reform coming into force as of 1994, Denmark has taken a number of measures in the same direction. It is fair to say, however, that these measures do not go as far as those in the three other countries.

3. Home mortgage interest can, of course, be seen differently, depending on whether or not the imputed income of the taxpayer's use of his own home is taxable. The Nordic countries have gradually abandoned their tradition of taxing this imputed income, but inasmuch as property taxes have been substituted for the tax on imputed rental income, it can still be argued that mortgage interest payments should in principle be deducted.

insurance capital (while kept in the insurance institution) and deduction for the contributions paired with taxability of the future insurance payments. With sufficiently low tax on the insurance institution, it was also attractive to invest in capital insurance, with no deduction for the premium payments, but also no tax on the ultimate pay-out.

Once it became apparent that a significant number of taxpayers in the higher brackets systematically used the interest deduction for "tax arbitrage" purposes, legislators found it necessary, first of all, to set a ceiling for the tax reduction offered by the interest deduction. A dual income tax rate, with the progressive surtax applying to an income base before interest deduction, could limit the value of the interest deduction to a less tempting amount than yielded by the 70-80 percent that was previously applied – a rate of 50 percent was expected to dampen the interest in tax arbitrage. These measures, however, fell short of the success expected of them.

Another similar problem had to do with the tax planning opportunities offered by the possibility of deducting current deficits incurred in side activities from the yield of the taxpayer's mainstream activity. An analysis of the facts behind some conspicuous cases of "zero tax returns" showed that not only interest arbitrage was used for this purpose, but also tax planning involving business ventures promising initial current losses, made up for later by capital gains. The use of flaws in the tax law, such as the double deduction of current losses in a partnership and a capital loss on the shares, was seen as one such issue. Of course the threat lingered that deductions reducing this year's tax base would be made up for by profits or gains realized once the taxpayer had been able to move his residence abroad, thus escaping the tax claim of the country he left.

Another important category of deductible losses were hobby losses. Tax administrations in the Nordic countries genuinely tried to tax hobby farmers by a correct evaluation of the benefits in kind from their country estates. The success was not great, however. In the case of horses, the issue was when to disregard the loss as a hobby loss; most of the time, the result was to refuse the one-horse owner his loss deduction, while at the same time to agree to the deduction claim of the owner of a whole stable.

Facing these issues, the Nordic countries have more or less abandoned the ideal of a synthetic, global income tax, settling for a system less inviting to tax avoidance and tax arbitrage. The system found suitable in this respect has two features. First of all, the general right to deduct losses has been severely curtailed, particularly with respect to hobby losses and losses incurred in what, with a US-inspired oxymoron, is called "passive activity," but also with respect to business losses incurred by taxpayers with positive employment income. Second, the income tax has been turned into a dual tax, establishing a progressive tax with personal exemptions for earned income, and a proportional tax with no such exemptions for income from capital, including more consistently than before even capital gains. It is worth mentioning that the new system is of recent date in all the countries and cannot yet be viewed as being well established.[4]

The following sections will deal with the dual income tax feature of the reforms, leaving aside the treatment of hobby losses, passive activities, etc.. The focus will be on the practical implications of trying to give logical coherence to a system of differential tax treatment of capital income and earned income, i.e. a dual income tax. First under study will be the Swedish example; the final section will cover the developments in Norway, Finland, and to some extent Denmark.

II. THE BASIC ISSUE

The Swedish example, as it materialized in the context of the 1991 tax reform, implied, first of all, a separation of "capital income" from "earned income," the former category including not only interest and dividends, but also capital gains and rental income from private homes.[5] The earned income is taxed after deduction from the base of a personal exemption.[6] There is a progressive rate – in the sense that the personal exemption is much lower for local government income tax than for central government tax, although for both taxes the rate as such is

4. In Sweden, a statutory change effective as of 1994 again offered a limited opportunity of deducting from employment income the initial losses incurred in an active business, but the 1991 rule of non-deductibility was reinstated as of January 1, 1995, only to be taken up for reconsideration some months later.

5. The traditional Swedish system of taxing the imputed income from the taxpayer's own residence has been abandoned in favor of a tax on real property, including, perhaps more on paper than in reality, a real property tax on private homes abroad.

6. The exemption is fixed at 25 percent of the "basic amount," a concept used in connection both with tax provisions and social security payments, and currently set at about SEK 37,500 (US$ 5,000). To make matters more complicated, the exemption is increased by 25 percent of the part of the income exceeding 0.86 but not more than 2.89 basic amounts, only to be reduced again by 10 percent of the amount by which the income exceeds 3.04 basic amounts until a minimum of 0.25 basic amounts is reached (a typical computer age provision).

proportional (the local government income tax on average is now close to 32 percent, and the central government income tax used to be 20 percent but has been temporarily increased to 25 percent).[7]

Income from capital is subject to central government tax only, at a proportional rate of 30 percent, levied on all income with no personal exemption. Most of this tax, except tax on capital gains and on the rental income from private homes, is collected by withholding. The most important feature of this new proportional tax is the treatment of negative income from capital. In the preparatory stages of the great tax reform, it was stated that the tax on capital income in general was a losing proposition, in as much as the tax forgone through the deduction of losses (mainly net debt interest) from gross income was larger than the revenue collected on positive income from capital. Even though the effect had already been mitigated by a 50 percent ceiling placed on the value of the loss deductions, the net result was still negative.

What happened in 1991 was that the relief for negative income from capital was reduced to a non-refundable tax credit of 30 percent of the first SEK 100,000 (roughly US$13,500), and 21 percent of the remaining negative income. The credit that cannot be used in one year cannot be carried forward to later years, nor carried back to earlier ones.

While this measure did not make the capital income tax a source of revenue, it did take away the previous incentive to households to borrow and spend. The result was stupendous in the form of increased household savings, particularly in the form of reduced mortgage and consumer credits. Still, when the new government presented its first tax bill in the fall of 1994, the estimated revenue effect of <u>not</u> (as previously had been planned) <u>reducing</u> the capital income tax rate from 30 to 25 percent, although small, had to be listed with a minus sign.[8]

---

7. Again, to make things more complicated, there is a double exemption from income subject to central government income tax: first comes the exemption amount established for municipal income tax purposes, and then comes what is called a bracket limit, established at SEK 170,000 for 1990 incomes, indexed so as to reach SEK 203,900 (about $ 27,200) for 1995 incomes. There is also a lump-sum central government tax of SEK 100, payable by all whose income above the municipal exemption is at least SEK 100.

8. The non-socialist government in power from 1991 to 1994 intended to reduce the capital income tax rate in general from 30 to 25 percent, but was prevented from doing so by a crisis deal with the social-democratic opposition – until it was forced out of office in 1994. Similarly, the implementation of the decision to abolish the net wealth tax was postponed, with the result that the tax remained in force until formally reinstated by the next government.

How could this rate differentiation be motivated? Technically, the explanation is simple. In the course of the preparation of the tax reform, designers had thoroughly studied and finally dismissed indexation of the tax base, mainly on grounds of simplification.[9] The upshot was that the capital income tax rate was set at a level playing rough justice to the need for indexation. The arithmetic was more than simple: assuming a 10 percent interest rate and a 4 percent inflation rate, a 30 percent tax on nominal interest will correspond to a 50 percent rate on the real interest, the latter roughly corresponding to the top marginal tax rate on earned income (i.e. at the time 30 percent local government tax plus 20 percent central government tax).[10]

Two ways now exist in which this rate differentiation requires differentiating measures affecting businesses.[11] One has to do with closely held corporations. The corporate income tax was reduced in the course of the reform to 30 percent, and later lowered to 28 percent, effective as of 1994. The classical system of taxing corporate profits and dividends was maintained, making for a cumulative tax burden on distributed profits of 51 (49.6) percent, if all net-of-tax profits are distributed.[12] In other words, if the owner of a closely-held corporation could choose freely between taking out a dividend and drawing the same amount as salary, his choice under the new system would be in

9. To be sure, the kind of indexation that takes the form of adjustment of exemptions and bracket limits was maintained. With respect to the tax base, however, even the modest degree of indexation existing before the reform, applying to capital gains, was abolished in favor of a general reduction of the rate of tax.

10. In his brilliant essay "From the Global Income Tax to the Dual Income Tax: Recent Tax Reforms in the Nordic Countries," 1 *International Tax and Public Finance* 57 (May 1994), Peter Birch Sørensen gives a much more profound account of the reasons for the differentiation, including at least one that would have made the hair rise on the heads of the Swedish politicians: "... if the philosophy of the comprehensive income tax is taken seriously, there is indeed a theoretical argument for taxing labor income at a higher rate than capital income, in contrast to popular beliefs." What he is driving at is the obvious failure of any tax system to cover the unrealized gains on human capital. To be sure, even the unrealized gains on real capital hardly lend themselves to effective capital gains tax.

11. The main source of wisdom on this matter is the 1973-1993 "Jubilee Publication" of the Nordic Council for Tax Research, "Tax Reform in the Nordic Countries," *IUSTUS*, Gothenburg 1993. An excellent summary of the issues is offered by Sven-Olof Lodin in his pamphlet, "The Nordic Reforms of Company and Shareholder Taxation – a Comparison," *Federation of Swedish Industries*, Stockholm 1994, an English translation of his Festschrift article for Edward Andersson (*Jurisdiska Föreningens i Finland Tidskrift* Nr. 5-6, 1993). The most profound work in the area is regrettably in Norwegian, Ole Gjems Onstad's "Delingsreglene" (The Division Rules), *ad Notam*, Gyldendal, Oslo, 1993. On Denmark, the recent textbook by Ole Bjørn, Lida Hulgaard, Aage Michelsen, and Margrethe Nørgaard, "Lærebog om indkomstskat" (Textbook on Income Tax), *Jurist- og Økonomforbundets Forlag*, 1994, is helpful – the character of the system of rules makes such help necessary.

12. This percentage is computed as 30(28) percent corporate income tax and 30 percent capital income tax on the remainder, assumed to be distributed as a dividend, or together 51(49.6) percent.

favor of the dividend (the salary would carry the full income tax plus social security contributions, payroll tax, etc.). Accordingly, rules had to be found for setting a limit to what could be treated as income from capital. Moreover, if the shares of the corporation were sold, the capital gain could be deemed to represent accumulated personal earned income of the shareholder, and this accumulated compensation should in principle be taxed as income from labor rather than as a capital gain taxable at the lower (30 percent) rate.

In contrast, if the owner of the business chose to run it as a proprietary firm or as a partnership, there would be a tax disadvantage inasmuch as the whole profit would be regarded as earned income, taxed (at the margin) at around 51 percent. The opportunity for a corporation to retain profits taxable at only 30 (28) percent would not be available to the proprietary firm or the partnership.

III. THE SOLUTIONS

III.1 The closely-held corporations

The problems of separating labor income from capital income, in closely-held corporations as well as in proprietorships, were not solved consistently and in one operation, but at different times and according to different principles.

Concerning closely-held corporations, the 1991 tax reform produced an initial set of rules known as 3 § 12 mom SIL.[13] The point of departure was the capital invested. A dividend representing a normal yield on this capital was accepted as a genuine dividend and taxed accordingly. Any dividend payment in excess of this norm was seen as earned income, and taxable as such, albeit with the difference that social

13. References to Swedish tax law are made with the Swedish connotation, "SIL" standing for the central government income tax law, and "KL" for the local government income tax law. A closely-held corporation (32 § anvp 14 KL) is defined as a corporation in which a minimum of 50 percent of the shares is held by one or a few individuals. Active shareholders may together count as one person (so as to make professional corporations like law-firms and medical offices fall under the rules). Only those who themselves (or related persons) are or (during the last ten years) have been active in the enterprise, are affected. If it can be shown that outsiders have a substantive right to dividends (in practice, 30 percent), the rules do not apply, since it is not expected to be profitable to change salary into dividends if the cost involved includes splitting the money with outside shareholders who take 30 percent or more. The definition of related persons is broad, including parents, grandparents, spouses, descendants and their spouses, siblings, inlaws, nephews and nieces, and estates of any of these. Even step- and foster-children are listed.

security contributions and payroll tax were not paid, whereas the salary part of the dividend, like dividends in general, was not deductible. The rules establishing this system were certainly not simple.

The capital could be computed either on the basis of the indexed original acquisition cost of the shares, or taken as their value at the end of 1990, adjusted for the undervaluation prescribed for certain business assets in the context of the assessment for net wealth tax purposes of shares in closely-held companies. The indexation did not include periods before 1970 or after 1990. The interest rate was the government borrowing rate plus 5 percent. Profits retained in the corporation could be added to basis and could also be distributed a later year as part of the "permitted" dividend.

In 1994 a modification was made, adding to these rules a new law (SFS 1994: 775) that established rules for computing the capital base of closely-held corporations, the shares of which were acquired before 1992, and allowed this computation to be used as an alternative to the historic purchase cost of the shares. The capital base is measured on the basis of the balance sheet at the end of fiscal year 1992.

Moreover, at the same time, a new subsection was introduced (3 § 12a mom SIL), establishing the right of a closely-held corporation to use as a basis for computing the permitted dividend not just the capital value, as computed under the historic purchasing cost rule, but also 10 percent of the total payroll (to the extent it exceeded ten "basic amounts"), placing the threshold at approximately US$ 50,000. Unused dividends under this rule (dividends retained) may be carried forward to later years. Moreover, the owner must have taken out a salary representing at least 150 percent of the compensation offered to the highest paid employee on the payroll. Salaries to shareholders do not qualify.[14]

As to capital gains, the procedure (again established under 3 § 12 mom SIL) is different. Once the capital gain has been computed, the splitting up into capital gain and earned income takes place in two steps. First, an amount corresponding to dividends retained is taxed as capital gain. Second, half of the rest of the total capital gain is taxed as such, the other half as earned income. There is a maximum, defined as 100 times

---

14. The provision is too limited to mean much, tax-wise. Yet it is of special theoretical interest, inasmuch as it shows a non-socialist government subscribing after a fashion to the "Mehrwert" (value added) theory of Karl Marx. Part of the payroll is seen as flowing to the capitalist as the yield of his capital rather than as a result of his own work! Norway has developed a similar rule.

the "basic amount" (approximately US$ 500,000), that must be taxed as earned income, any excess being added to the capital gains part.

III.2 THE ABOLITION OF THE CLASSICAL SYSTEM

Once, in late 1993, taking effect as of 1994 but reversed by the new government one year thereafter, the classical system of double taxation was abandoned: dividends paid on Swedish shares to Swedish residents were simply made tax exempt. The thought behind this was that an integrated system with a tax credit for underlying corporate tax would be meaningless if the dividend income would be subject anyhow to a proportional tax rate close to the corporate tax rate.[15] The need was felt even more strongly in this situation to remove the temptation of disguising earned income as dividends. More restrictions were placed on the size of the dividend from a closely held corporation that could be booked as a dividend rather than as earned income.[16]

Tax rules for capital gains also changed. Share value accretion based on retained profits should be dealt with, it was felt, using the same principles applicable to profits, had they been distributed. The government would have preferred to apply the Norwegian "RISK" method, which increases the capital gains tax cost base by the amount of profits retained.[17] Pending a further study of the practicability of such a system, the capital gains tax rate on shares was halved. Since it had already been reduced to 25 percent as a first step in a planned (but never realized) general reduction of the capital income tax rate from 30

---

15. It is fair to say that the former government failed in its task to bring it home to the voters on the left side that dividend income was not exempted by the reform; rather it was taxed just once, but at the level of the corporation. The parallel, of course, was interest income, deductible at the corporate level and taxed at the lender's level. Norway and Finland went through the rigmarole of taxing the dividend income with full credit for underlying corporate tax (imputation system) to achieve the same result, i.e. typically no tax on the shareholder, yet without voter protests from the left.

16. The 1993 government (rightly) feared that the abolition of the classical system might prove to be a passing incident, the old system being restored by a new government. For that reason, they took great care to ensure that corporations of all categories would abstain from an abusive orgy in dividend distributions during what they might consider to be a one-time opportunity to avoid the rule of double taxation. Accordingly, a series of maximum rules was included in the tax law. The rules separating dividend and earned income in the case of closely-held corporations obviously greatly reduced the beneficial effect of the integration rule on this category of shareholders.

17. The acronym "RISK" has nothing to do with risk aversion but stands for "Regulering av Inngangsverdien med Skattlagd Inntekt" (Adjustment of the Basis with Taxed Profits). The 1992 US Treasury study of the integration issue toys with the same idea.

to 25 percent, the rate was now 12.5 percent. With the purpose of achieving the same tax burden as before on the amount of a capital gain deemed to be earned income, the rule was changed so as to allocate 70 percent of the gain (after deduction of retained profits and the indexation amount) to earned income.

The double taxation of distributed profits was reintroduced effective January 1, 1995, and the capital gains tax rate on shares was increased from 12.5 to 30 percent. In this context, the 50/50 split was reintroduced. At the time of this writing, trustworthy rumors have it that in a political deal between the government and the center (former farmers') party, an integrated system has been tentatively agreed upon, allowing credit for underlying corporate income tax against capital income tax on dividends paid by unquoted corporations. (Given a corporate tax rate of 28 percent and a capital income tax rate of 30 percent, this would reduce the net income tax payable by the shareholder to 2 percent.) Indications are that this move, if at all realized, is supposed to need some detailed preparation and could be legislated on only in late 1995.

III.3 THE PROPRIETARY FIRMS

The problem remained, however, of how to deal with the proprietary firms. On their part, they also experienced, first of all, the issue of separating labor income from capital income. If capital income in general was subject to a proportional, low tax, then an argument could be made for allowing owners of proprietary firms and partnerships to be taxed at the same rate on the yield of their invested capital. With respect to the deduction of debt interest, a similar issue came up with respect to the opportunity open to those carrying on an active business, to deduct as business cost those interest payments that might in fact be related to assets other than those of the business.

Another issue was that the competitive situation between corporations and proprietary firms (and partnerships) was seen as distorted by the fact that corporations could retain profits taxed at the corporate rate (30 percent in the 1991 reform, reduced to 28 percent as of 1994). In contrast, owners of proprietary firms and shareholders in partnerships might have to pay not only a marginal income tax of somewhere over 50 percent, but also social security contributions to the tune of some 30 percent (deductible from income) on top of it.

One solution to these problems – extensively studied in the preparatory works for the 1991 tax reform, although finally dismissed – was the "fence method," under which owners of proprietary firms and partnerships could opt for corporate treatment of profits not taken out of the business. The reason for dismissing this idea may have been fear that its complication would irritate even those taxpayers in whose interest the rule would be enacted.

The second part of the former issue was, however, dealt with already in the context of the 1991 tax reform, namely through the introduction of a specific rule on how to allocate interest costs (44 § KL). The basic rule was one of tracing, with an alternative rule prescribing separation in proportion to asset values.

The rule did not work satisfactorily. Moreover, it did not satisfy the need to distinguish positive capital income from business profits. Therefore, in 1993, effective 1994, a new law was enacted, the "Law on division of interest at taxation" (SFS 1993:1536) establishing the principle of setting apart interest income, both in a positive and in a negative sense.

The rules governing positive splitting prescribe that the government borrowing rate plus 3 percentage points be applied to the net value of the business at the beginning of the fiscal year. The principle is simply to allow as much of the total profit as corresponds to this amount to be taxed under the rules for income from capital. If the profit is not sufficient to cover the whole amount, the rest may be carried forward. Also, the taxpayer may opt out of the income-splitting method (he may wish to have more earned income credited to his account for social security purposes).

The negative splitting is the opposite, i.e. if the book value of the firm or the partnership is negative, the negative net value is multiplied, in this case by the government borrowing rate plus one percentage point. This amount is accounted for as business profit, whereas a corresponding deduction is made under income from capital. (As was mentioned earlier, the net loss under income from capital gives rise to a tax credit equal to 30 percent of the loss for the first SEK 100,000 and 21 percent for the rest). There is a *de minimis* rule, division being made only if the amount exceeds SEK 50,000 (US$ 6,700).

Numerous detailed rules prescribe how to compute the value of the assets and debts, not least with regard to the treatment of book reserves and the like.

A solution to the second problem, how to deal with profits retained in the business, was found in 1993, in the form of a special tax on "expansion funds," which would bear the same rate as the corporate income tax. This tax could be levied, as an alternative to the personal income tax on the proprietor's earned income, on profits set aside for the purpose of expanding the business. The technique used was set out in a separate law on "expansion funds" (SFS 1993:1537). The main rule is that money may be set aside by owners of proprietary firms or partnerships, and a deduction can be taken for purposes of income tax (and social security contributions). Instead, another tax, the tax on expansion funds ("expansionsmedelsskatt"), is paid at a rate of 28 percent. If the funds are brought back to profits and earnings, they are subject to regular income tax and social security contributions, but the tax on expansion funds paid earlier is now refunded. It is worth noting that in the absence of a provision for the carry-back of losses, the expansion funds (and for that matter also the so-called `period equalization reserves' that we are not discussing here) can be said to be an effective substitute.

The limit for this set-off is first of all that the deduction must not give rise to a loss. A second limit is intended to ensure that the expansion funds are, indeed, kept in the business and not used for personal consumption purposes. This is achieved by a ceiling rule, establishing that 72 percent of the expansion funds may not exceed the net capital as computed for purposes of the division of capital income, with positive adjustment for such a loss that has not been deductible from other income, and with negative adjustment for added new capital. Also, for partnerships, there is a rule preventing the set-off to reduce the value of a share below zero.

While these rules no doubt were conceived in the best interest of the taxpayers concerned, their complication certainly tests the capacity of the taxpayers and their advisors as well as of the tax authorities. Recently, complaints have been heard that small and medium enterprises find it unworkable to understand the provisions themselves, too expensive to hire experts who do, and not realistic to expect the revenue service to cope with them, either.

IV. OTHER NORDIC EXPERIENCES

IV.1 Norway

The leading nation in the field is Norway. Norway, as well as Sweden and Finland, makes a clear distinction between proportionately taxed capital income (28 percent tax) and earned income (taxed progressively, at a rate of up to 63.8 percent, including social security tax). One motive for the differentiation is the net wealth tax. That tax was not used as an argument in Sweden, possibly because they decided to abolish it – the retraction made by the new government in 1994, before it was to be implemented.

The main difference in approach between Norway and Sweden is that Sweden attaches the splitting-rule (separating capital income from labor income) in the closely-held corporation context in the event of a dividend payment or the realization of a capital gain on the shares of an active shareholder or a related person. In contrast, Norway expects the splitting to be done every year, both for corporations and proprietary firms. The necessary condition for a splitting to take place is that the activity of the taxpayer is active, not passive. Moreover, if one or more outsiders hold a third or more of the shares, the rules are rendered inapplicable.

In Norway the concept of related persons is narrower than it is in Sweden -- siblings are not supposed to be related, something that experience tells may sometimes correspond to the facts and sometimes not. The rules do not apply if the active shareholders are 23 or more, none of them having more than 3 percent of the shares. Moreover, the rule providing a ceiling for the earned income part of a capital gain implies that splitting cannot result in an amount exceeding 34 basic amounts to be taxed as earned income. This rule is similar to the 100 basic amounts rule limiting the earned income part of a capital gain in Sweden.

The Norwegian rule permits treatment as capital yield of total profits an amount of no less than 16 percent of the capital value. This quite often implies that there is no earned income left, once the capital yield part has been taxed as such. If, however, there is still some earned income to be taxed, there might be a deduction from the part of income being assumed to be earned income–this time based on the payroll amount. The maximum deduction is 12 percent of the payroll, covering employees other than shareholders. Since the difference between the rate on earned income and the rate on income from capital is 23.7 percent, the net saving is 2.8 percent of payroll. The deduction may, however, not reduce the earned income of the highest paid shareholder below 145 percent of the best-paid non-shareholder employee.

The Norwegian rules are intended as a sort of trial run – something that has been criticized as callous with respect to the many taxpayers involved, who have had to learn the new rules and adapt to them. It is, however, from the perspective of the Nordic neighbors, impressive to note the thoroughness by which the Norwegian lawmakers have attacked even the most minute problems involved in this system.

IV.2 Finland

As in the Swedish system, the profit-splitting rules in Finland focus on the distribution stage only. Different from the Swedish system, the Finnish system allows no splitting with respect to capital gains, only the distribution of dividends. Hence, they open the door for transforming progressively taxed earned income of active shareholders into capital gains, taxed proportionately at 25 percent, whereas the maximum marginal rate on earned income exceeds 62 percent. The splitting rule applies to corporate businesses, but there are detailed rules to provide relief even to private firms, farms, and partnerships.

One point at which the Finnish rule might open a loophole is that the capital base is computed on the basis of each new year's balance sheet. Hence, by retaining profits, instead of taking them out as salary, active shareholders can reduce the share of profits to be taxed as earned income in the future. The yield ratio is 15 percent of the asset value in the latest balance sheet, and the splitting rule is applied not just to dividends paid to active shareholders, but to all dividends.

IV.3 Denmark

Denmark has also made a distinction between capital income and earned income, but less rigorously than its Nordic neighbors. All types of income are subject to some kind of rate progression, and this applies to dividend income as well. For dividends, the basic rate is 30 percent (that will be reduced to 25 in 1996), but annual dividends exceeding DKK 31,700 in 1993 (around US$ 5,300) are taxed at 40 percent. A distinction is made between positive and negative income from capital, with the intention of reducing the marginal effect of the latter, while keeping the progression on the former.

The Danish rules allow proprietary firms to choose between regular taxation of the profits as earned income, and a different system implying a separate tax computation for the business profits, with taxation of profits withdrawn as if they were interest. This reminds one strongly of the "fence method" discussed earlier. The element of optional treatment is striking, the regime chosen can be changed every year.

V. CONCLUSION

The Nordic countries currently provide an interesting test laboratory for theoretically ingeniously conceived but practically extremely complicated systems of separating capital and earned income. It is an open issue whether the final judgment on these systems should be based on theoretical arguments or on practical experience. They will probably earn high marks on the former, and meet much criticism on the latter.

TAXATION OF THE SELF-EMPLOYED UNDER A DUAL INCOME TAX

PETER B. SØRENSEN

Economic Policy Research Unit, Copenhagen

and

KÅRE P. HAGEN

Norwegian School of Economics and Business Administration

I. INTRODUCTION

In almost all countries operating a personal income tax, the taxation of income from self-employment raises a host of conceptual and practical problems.

Some of the classical problems relate to the measurement of income. For instance, in certain lines of business such as agriculture, in which self-employment is important, income in-kind may constitute an important part of total income. As another example, it is often difficult to draw the dividing line between legitimate business expenses (which should be deductible from taxable income) and expenditure for private consumption purposes (which should not be deductible).

Still, while the problem of income measurement may be quantitatively more important in the area of self-employment, it is not conceptually different from the problem of measuring the net income of wage earners. This paper will therefore focus on another classical issue involved in the taxation of the self-employed: How does one ensure that income from self-employment, income from employment (wage income), and income from incorporated firms are all treated equally by the tax code?

If governments were able and willing to implement an ideal Schanz-Haig-Simons comprehensive income tax, this problem would not arise. A comprehensive income tax would subject all types of income to the same personal income tax schedule, with no tax differentiation between the various sources of income. This would also hold for corporate source income, since all corporate profits would be attributed to the individual shareholders and taxed in their hands. However, the total tax burden on corporate profits, in practice, typically deviates from the personal income tax rate of the shareholder because the corporate income tax is not fully integrated with the personal income tax. The corporate income tax rate is, thus, often considerably lower than the top marginal tax rate on personal income, and the taxation of (accrued) capital gains on shares is frequently rather lenient. Under these circumstances, the owners of a corporation would be able to accumulate profits within the firm on more favorable tax terms than would a proprietor. For this reason, it has sometimes been argued that profits retained in unincorporated firms should receive the same favorable tax treatment as profits retained within a corporation; this idea, indeed, has exerted some influence on tax policy in the Nordic countries.

Another potential inequity arises from the fact that capital income may be taxed at a lower rate than the (top) marginal tax rate on income from labor. This may be because social security taxes are usually levied only on labor income, but in the Nordic countries it is also due to the fact that recent tax reforms have introduced a separate low flat rate of tax on capital income, as described in Sørensen (1994). Since part of the income of a sole proprietor must be considered as a return on the capital he has invested in his firm, it would seem inequitable if this income were taxed at the high marginal rates applying to labor income.

Against this background, the present paper discusses whether it is in fact desirable and feasible to eliminate tax discrimination between wage earners, the self-employed, and (the owners of) corporations. In the theoretical Part II of the paper, we discuss whether economic efficiency would indeed require a tax system that is neutral with respect to the organization of economic activity. Thus, section II.1 questions whether it is efficient to tax the return to real assets in the same way, regardless of whether they are held by a private firm or by a corporation, while section II.2 questions whether the return to human capital should be taxed at the same rate regardless of whether the owner invests his human wealth in his own firm or chooses to sell the services of his human capital to an employer via the labor market. We conclude that, although efficiency does not necessarily call for a tax system that is completely neutral along the dimensions mentioned here, the case for systematic tax differentiation across different organizational forms is weak, given our present theoretical knowledge. Furthermore, leaving efficiency issues aside, the time-honored principle of "horizontal equity" -- which obviously calls for tax neutrality -- still seems to have considerable appeal.

Parts III and IV therefore proceed to discuss how the tax system could be designed so as to ensure that income from self-employment is given the same tax treatment as income from incorporated firms and income from employment. The discussion centers around two different methods of taxing the self-employed. According to the so-called "Fence-model," income retained in the firm is taxed more leniently than income that is distributed to the owner. By contrast, the so-called "Source-model" splits the total business income of the self-employed into a labor income component and a capital income component, with the purpose of applying different tax rates to the two types of income. We argue in Part III that the "Fence-model" has certain drawbacks from the perspectives of efficiency and equity. Part IV therefore focuses on problems of designing a "Source-model" that will meet the criterion of tax neutrality under the new system of separate taxation of income from capital and labor that has been applied in the Nordic countries.

In Part V of the chapter we then consider how the four major Nordic countries have actually chosen to tax income from self-employment after the recent tax reforms. Since the problems of taxing income from small corporations in which the owners take active part in the management of the firm are in many respects similar to those of taxing income from self-employment, we also briefly describe the tax rules applied to corporations with "active" owners. Finally, Part VI summarizes our main findings.

II. TAXATION AND THE ORGANIZATION OF ECONOMIC ACTIVITY

II.1. Two dimensions of tax neutrality

The issue of tax neutrality with respect to the organization of economic activity has at least two dimensions. One is in relation to alternative forms of ownership of *physical* capital. Neutrality in this context would mean that the form of ownership does not affect the effective taxation of capital income generated by any given type of physical asset.

Second, part of the net business income of a self-employed individual represents a reward for his effort and skills and may thus be seen as the remuneration of the *human* capital which the owner invests in his firm. In part, the tax on business income is therefore a tax on the returns accruing to the owner's human capital. Neutrality in this dimension would mean that the effective tax burden on returns to human capital is the same whether this capital is employed in the owner's own firm or whether it is hired by other firms through the labor market.

Sections II.3 and II.4 will discuss the efficiency case for having a business income tax that is neutral along these dimensions. To provide a background to this discussion, we must identify the main economic characteristics of the different organizational forms and the trade-offs involved in choosing between them. This is the subject of the next section.

II.2. Economic characteristics of alternative organizational forms

Our discussion will focus on three alternative organizational forms:[18] (i) Sole proprietorships, (ii) Closely held private corporations ("closed corporations," for brevity), and (iii) Public corporations listed on the stock exchange ("open" corporations). Since our arguments relating to sole proprietorships carry over with only slight modifications to partnerships, this form of ownership is also implicitly covered by our analysis.

From an economic perspective, the crucial characteristic of *proprietorships* is that the economic functions of risk-bearing and management decision-making are concentrated in the same person. The

---

[18]. The analysis in this section borrows heavily from Fama and Jensen (1983.a,b).

proprietor is the firm's "residual claimant," since his remuneration is determined by the business income left over after all payments to other factors of production. At least as long as the proprietor is able to meet all his obligations, he thus carries all of the income risk associated with the productive activity undertaken by the firm. At the same time, he also makes all the management decisions affecting the net income accruing to the firm. Because all of the wealth effects of management decisionmaking are felt by the decisionmaker himself, no "agency" problem can arise from conflicts of interest between the managers and the owners of the firm. The fact that managerial incentives are thus "correct" may be seen as the main social benefit associated with proprietorships.

On the other hand, proprietorships involve two types of social costs (Fama and Jensen, 1983b, pp. 332-33): First, by investing (a considerable part of) his net wealth in a single firm, the proprietor forgoes the optimal portfolio diversification from which he might have gained by investing his wealth in the capital market. This implies a less efficient allocation of risk, increasing the cost of risk-bearing services and probably leading to less investment in projects with uncertain returns in the non-corporate sector. Second, the management decision process may suffer efficiency losses because sole proprietors will, to some extent, have been "recruited" among individuals with sufficient levels of wealth and willingness to bear risks, rather than among those with the highest management skills.

Formally, the switch from the organizational form of proprietorship to that of a *closed corporation* involves a switch from unlimited to limited liability. Other things equal, part of the income risk associated with the firm is thus shifted from equity holders to debt holders. This may improve risk allocation to the extent that debtholders are in a better position than the firm's equityholder(s) to diversify their risks. However, as stressed by Gordon and MacKie-Mason (1993, pp. 6-7), the limited liability of the owners of a corporation is only a "default" rule – defining the allocation of liabilities that are not otherwise allocated by explicit contracts. Normally, if a proprietorship or partnership is transformed into a closed corporation, the firm's debtholders will not passively accept the increase in the riskiness of their claims implied by the shift to limited liability. For instance, it is quite common that the shareholders of small corporations must pledge personal assets in order to obtain external bank financing. Essentially, such supplementary contracts requiring personal collateral may completely undo the formal shift to limited liability and the associated change in risk allocation, implying that the equityholder(s) of the firm continue to carry (almost) all of the risk. In that case it would seem that the allocation of risk is improved only insofar as the switch from sole proprietorship to the corporate ownership form is associated with a splitting of the firm's equity among several shareholders. Notice, however, that such risk-sharing does not require a switch to the corporate form of organization, since it could also be achieved by a change from sole proprietorship to the partnership form.

Of course, this conclusion regarding the unimportance of the formal switch to limited liability will have to be modified if the transactions costs of writing and enforcing the supplementary contracts are so substantial that they prevent the shift to limited liability from being "undone" through recontracting. In that case, some risk will in fact be shifted to debtholders, and *ceteris paribus* this is likely to induce a (slight) increase in the interest rate that the firm will have to pay on its debt.[19] From the perspective of the firm's equityholder(s), the decision to incorporate would then seem to involve a simple trading of risk (which is reduced by the shift to limited liability) for expected return (which is also reduced because of the higher cost of debt service). However, we believe that such a change in the owner's perceived trade-off between risk and return is likely to be of minor quantitative importance.

Just as the shift from proprietorship (or partnership) to the ownership structure of a closed corporation will hardly imply substantial improvements in risk allocation, it is also unlikely to lead to significant improvements in the quality of management unless the transition to corporate status happens to be associated with the appointment of professional managers. Casual observation suggests that this is not typically the case. Thus, it is quite common for (one of) the owners of a closed corporation to work as a manager in the firm. As an initial generalization, it would therefore appear that the organizational forms of proprietorships and closed corporations differ little from an economic viewpoint. At least this is true for closed corporations with so-

19. This does not necessarily imply that one will always observe a rise in the interest rate charged to the firm when it incorporates and full recontracting does not take place. If incorporation happens to be associated with a strengthening of the firm's equity base or with improved external monitoring of the firm's management, the perceived risk of lending to the firm (and hence the firm's cost of debt service) may actually fall.

called "active" owners taking part in the management of the firm. In short, in closed corporations it will typically be the case that the functions of risk-bearing and decisionmaking are both performed by the owners of the firm.

By contrast, *open (public) corporations* are usually characterized by the well-known "separation of ownership and control," since they are normally run by professional managers with special skills in decisionmaking. While these managers may hold some of the shares in the corporation, they rarely bear the major part of the wealth consequences of their decisions. Instead, these consequences are felt mainly by shareholders, who specialize in bearing risk but who take no part in management decisionmaking and who have only imperfect information on all of the factors and all of the management actions affecting the firm's profit stream.

The social benefits associated with the organizational form of public corporations arise from improved efficiency in decisionmaking. This improved efficiency can be attributed to the professionalization of management and to improved allocation of risks stemming from the fact that shares in the corporation are publicly traded, allowing shareholders to reap the gains from portfolio diversification. However, because of the separation of the management and risk-bearing functions combined with asymmetric information between shareholders and managers, and because managers and shareholders may have conflicting interests, the open corporation gives rise to certain agency costs that do not arise in proprietorships and closed corporations. Thus, to restrict the ability of corporate managers to deviate from stock market value-maximizing behavior, shareholders need to monitor the management. This involves some transactions costs, just as some efficiency may be lost in so far as deviations from value-maximizing behavior cannot be eliminated completely.[20]

The balance of costs and benefits associated with the different organizational forms will clearly differ across various sectors of the

[20]. It is worth noting that there are also agency problems associated with debt contracts. Indeed, the more intensive external monitoring of open corporations - due to auditing regulations and the incentives of the external equity market - may imply that the moral hazard problem giving rise to the agency costs of debt contracts is less severe in open corporations than it is in proprietorships and closed corporations. Empirically, bankruptcy frauds are more frequent for small firms under single ownership. Hence, the higher agency costs for equity holders in open corporations may be offset to some extent by lower agency costs for debtholders in these firms. This point was neglected by Fama and Jensen (1983a,b).

economy. In sectors where economies of scale are important, efficient production will often require complex large-scale operations implying high benefits from specialized management skills. In such sectors productive activity will also often require high aggregate risks and demand large amounts of wealth to be invested by the residual income claimants, thereby increasing the benefits that residual claimants may obtain from portfolio diversification. Thus, one would expect open corporations to be the dominant organizational form in such lines of business, whereas proprietorships and closed corporations can be expected to be more important in sectors that are not characterized by important economies of scale that lead to large demands for specialized management skills, specialized risk bearing, and wealth from residual claimants (Fama and Jensen, 1983b, pp. 332-33).

We would also expect that the balance of costs and benefits associated with different ownership structures could change significantly over the life cycle of an individual firm. In the early stages of the life cycle, when the scale of the firm's operations is still small, the cost-benefit calculus will almost always favor the organizational forms of proprietorships, partnerships, or closed corporations. The choice between these ownership structures and the switch between them will depend on the exact way in which the owners of the firm wish to divide risks and management responsibilities among themselves. If aggregate risks are high already from the upstart of the firm, this will tend to favor the corporate form of organization. Apart from tax considerations (to which we shall turn in the next section), other legal and practical considerations may also play an important role. For example, when a succession and the associated transfer of inheritance has to take place, the legal construct of a closed corporation may be better suited to deal with problems of indivisibilities of assets than might a proprietorship or partnership. The fact that the legal rights and obligations of the holders of debt and equity are usually more well defined and regulated will sometimes be seen as an advantage of the corporate form of organization, but circumstances may also exist in which the owner(s) of the firm prefer the non-corporate ownership form in order to gain the greater flexibility implied by the absence of such regulation.

When the firm is growing over time, the scale and complexity of its operations may reach a point where the open corporation becomes the most attractive organizational structure, due to increasing demands for specialized management skills and aggregate risk-taking. Before the firm "goes public," we would expect it to have already gone through the organizational stage of a closed corporation.

If the choice of organizational form is made by balancing the costs and benefits described above, the question for tax policy makers is whether – and possibly how – the tax system should interfere with this cost-benefit calculus. We now turn to this question.

II.2. Taxation of physical capital and organizational form

The standard efficiency argument for taxing the returns to physical capital independently of the ownership structure is that the required pre-tax rates of return on investment will then be independent of those who undertake the investment. Moreover, if the taxation on the investment side is neutral, required pre-tax rates of return will not only be the same across different categories of investors, but also across different assets, so that no increase in national income can be achieved by reallocating investment from one type of physical asset to another.[21]

While these observations provide a useful starting point for a discussion of the taxation of alternative organizational forms, they implicitly neglect the differences in risk allocation that characterize the different types of organization and the fact that an income tax will shift risk from the owners of risky firms to the taxpayers at large. Risk shifting through the tax system might be desirable from society's point of view if the private sector takes too little risk. That depends on how private risk relates to social risk. The undiversifiable social risk associated with an investment project is determined by the covariation between that project's risky income and total income in the economy. Undiversifiable private risk will be determined by the covariation with the returns of the stock market portfolio. With incomplete risk markets (e.g. because of problems related to moral hazard), the risk profile of the market portfolio would not be representative of the aggregate risk attached to national income, and one would expect that social risk would generally be lower than private risk. From that point of view, the

---

21. On the other hand, if various savers are taxed differently under the personal income tax, a neutral tax treatment of different assets would not necessarily contribute to increased economic efficiency if different savers own different assets, as in the segmented Miller equilibrium (Miller, 1977).

private sector is likely to be too risk averse. Risk shifting through the tax system may thus help bridge the gap between private and social risk.

As we have seen, proprietorships and closed corporations will tend to have higher costs of risk bearing, and will therefore tend to face a higher cost of equity capital than open corporations, because equityholders in open corporations do not have to bear diversifiable risks. In principle, the government is able to provide risk pooling through the income tax system, shifting part of the risk faced by the individual taxpayer to taxpayers at large, and replicating to some extent the possibilities for risk diversification offered by the stock market.[22] This insurance effect of the income tax will be stronger the higher the marginal tax rate and the greater the degree of tax progressivity. Because sole proprietors and the owners of closed corporations do not have the same opportunities for risk diversification as do the owners of open corporations, this might provide a case for taxing the income of proprietors and the owners of closed corporations at higher marginal rates than income from open corporations, which need less insurance.

Note that this is **not** an argument for having one set of tax rules for proprietors and another set of rules for all corporations, closed or open. Rather, our analysis suggests that one set of rules should pertain to proprietors and closed corporations ("small" firms), and another set to open corporations ("large" firms). This suggestion is based on the premise explained earlier that the switch from proprietorship to a closed corporation usually involves no qualitative change in the way risks and management responsibilities are allocated. If the two organizational forms are in fact close substitutes, there is no apparent reason why they should be subject to different tax rules.

Of course, one might argue that if proprietorships/partnerships and closed corporations are equally well suited to deal with the problems of resource allocation in the sector for small firms, there would be no distortions if the tax system were to treat them differently. Instead, the organizational form enjoying the most favorable tax treatment would simply tend to crowd out the less favored alternative, without any serious implications for the allocation of risks and managerial skills. However, as we suggested in the previous section,

22. The specific way in which risks are reallocated will of course depend on the way tax revenues are spent.

entrepreneurs may sometimes have good legal and practical reasons to prefer one organizational form over another. Thus, even though the two forms of organization may be close substitutes in most cases, some welfare loss will still exist from tax distortions to the choice between them as long as they are not perfect substitutes.[23]

To summarize the discussion so far, if the allocation of income risks in small firms is suboptimal, leading to a higher cost of equity capital in firms organized as proprietorships and closed corporations, a case may be made for providing such firms with some income insurance in the form of relatively high marginal tax rates. Furthermore, theoretical arguments exist that explain why it may be optimal to provide taxpayers with a choice between different tax schedules, if taxpayers have some private information about the returns to their effort and investment but are also uncertain about these returns (see Mirrlees [1990]). Such a choice may be provided by facing different ownership structures with different tax schedules and letting taxpayers choose between them. Still, these policy prescriptions are at most tentative and must be interpreted with great care, once the following additional factors are taken into account:

Credit rationing and marginal versus average tax rates. If a higher *marginal* tax rate on income from small firms also implies a higher *average* tax rate on such income, the ability of small firms to generate equity capital through retention of after-tax profits will be reduced. Insofar as these firms are subject to credit rationing, such a weakening of equity capital formation may cause a further reduction of investment in small enterprises in a situation in which investment in that sector has already been discouraged by a relatively high cost of equity capital. We stress, therefore, that our analysis provides no case for a relatively high average tax rate on the return to the physical capital invested in small firms. If anything, it suggests that the average tax rate on such income should be somewhat lower, whereas the marginal tax rate should be somewhat higher than the corresponding average and marginal tax rates on other forms of income.

Moral hazard. If the tax system provides a high degree of income insurance through high marginal tax rates and liberal loss-offset

23. The inter-sectoral distortions stemming from tax discrimination between proprietorships and closed corporations with active owners will clearly be magnified when there are legal restrictions on the choice of organizational form in some sectors. As an example of such restrictions, Danish law prohibits enterprises in the primary agricultural sector from being organized as corporations.

provisions, this insurance may weaken the incentives for entrepreneurs to manage their firms so as to avoid large losses. This is the well-known trade-off between insurance and incentives – a tradeoff that obviously limits the optimal level of insurance. As stressed by Arnott and Stiglitz (1991), the provision of non-market insurance may also crowd out some market insurance, thereby limiting the extent to which the government is able to improve risk-spreading.

The insurance function of a proportional income tax. Even if the income from all types of organizations were taxed at a uniform proportional rate, the introduction of such a tax would still increase the relative attractiveness (in expected utility terms) of the more risky income flows, as demonstrated in the appendix. Consequently, even if income from self-employment were not subject to a higher marginal tax rate than other forms of income, we might still expect the insurance effect of a uniform "neutral" tax system to shift some additional resources into the sector for small firms, relative to the no-tax situation.

II.3. Taxation of the self-employed and returns to human capital

While part of the net business income of a self-employed individual represents remuneration of entrepreneurial risk and returns to the equity-financed physical capital invested in the firm, the remaining part constitutes returns to his human capital, that is, compensation for the work, effort and skills which he puts into his business. The effective taxation of this income from human capital will depend on the definition of the business income tax base and on the statutory business income tax rate.

Instead of employing his human capital for his own firm, the owner could "lease" it to other firms through the labor market. In that case the returns to his human capital would accrue as wage income and would also be taxed as such. For example, a carpenter may work for a construction firm as a laborer and have his income taxed as wage income, or he may establish his own firm, in which case his income would be taxed as business income. Similarly, a tax lawyer may work as an employee in a tax consulting firm, or he may establish his own firm, in which case he would be considered as self-employed by the tax authorities.

One dimension of the tax neutrality issue is, then, whether the tax burden on human capital should be the same when this form of capital is employed in the owner's own business and when it is hired by other employers through the labor market. If the tax system offers tax advantages to the human capital of the self-employed, this will create incentives for transforming wage income into business income through establishing one's own firm and offering labor services as various kinds of contractor activities. Apart from the distributional effects of this sort of tax planning, the differential tax treatment of proprietor income and wage income may cause real allocative effects if there is a real resource cost to the setting up of firms, and if the labor productivity of the owner depends on whether he works for others in an employee-employer relationship or whether he is self-employed.

The human capital of the self-employed individual can partly be considered as mobile capital that could be employed equally productively in other firms, and partly as firm-specific human capital in the form of special entrepreneurial skills and effort. The taxation of business income will, to some extent, be a tax on returns to this firm-specific capital. How these returns should be taxed from an efficiency point of view will depend on the supply elasticity of firm-specific human capital. If entrepreneurial firm-specific skills and effort are supplied inelastically, the returns to this type of human capital are in the nature of pure rents and could then be taxed away without causing real distortions, while an elastic supply would call for a more lenient tax treatment.

One might expect that the labor input of the owner is normally more productively employed in the owner's own business, partly because it is likely to be complementary to the firm-specific human capital, and partly because the incentives would be better when a person is working for himself instead of working for others. Whether this should have any consequences for the taxation of the self-employed depends on the efficiency of the capital market with regard to the establishment of owner-managed unincorporated firms. One could perhaps point to information asymmetries between external financiers and entrepreneurs hampering the establishment of firms exploiting the owner's specific entrepreneurial skills and know-how. Hence, entrepreneurs may be rationed in the capital market in their attempt to employ their skills in the most productive way. Whether this possible distortion should be remedied through the tax system depends on whether the information asymmetry is a less serious problem for the tax authorities than for the capital market. Here the burden of proof probably lies with those advocating that this imperfection should be corrected through the tax system.[24]

The return to human capital is risky because the demand for labor services varies as a result of short-run fluctuations in business activity, as well as structural changes in the economy. When the owner is employed in his own firm, he will have to absorb all of this risk himself. By contrast, when he is employed as a worker, part of the risk will normally be borne by the employer. Hence, the net income of the self-employed will generally be more risky than the income of wage earners. Owners of human capital must thus trade off the insurance offered by employment contracts against the gains in expected income that might be obtained whenever human capital can be more productively employed in the owner's own business.

This trade-off between insurance (improved risk allocation) and productivity is rather similar to that encountered in the taxation of the returns to physical capital under alternative organizational forms. Thus, employers – and in particular the owners of large open corporations – may be better positioned to absorb the risk associated with the employment of human capital because they may have better opportunities for risk diversification. Hence, the utilization of the owner's human capital in a sole proprietorship may involve a suboptimal risk allocation. To the extent that the government is able to pool risks via the tax system, thereby replicating in part the risk spreading undertaken by private employers, this could provide a case for offering income insurance through a relatively high marginal tax rate on income from self-employment combined with liberal loss-offset provisions for such income. Again, however, the modifications mentioned in the previous section should be kept in mind: First, our analysis provides no argument for a relatively high *average* tax rate on the returns to the human capital of the self-employed. Second, a high degree of income insurance through the tax system may crowd out some private insurance and exacerbate certain moral hazard problems by weakening managerial incentives to avoid large losses. Third, if the individual is risk averse and is indifferent between self-employment and

24. Section III.3 briefly discusses whether the existence of credit rationing provides a case for government intervention.

work in the labor market in the pre-tax situation, and if income attainable through self-employment is more risky than the alternative wage income, a uniform proportional income tax with full loss-offset provisions would favor the more risky alternative and would thus in itself tend to shift economic activity in favor of self-employment.

II.4. Implications for tax policy

The two previous sections suggested that it is not necessarily efficient to tax income earned by proprietors and the owners of closely held corporations according to the same rules as income from large open corporations, once it is recognized that these alternative organizational forms involve different allocations of risks and management skills. Indeed, our analysis suggested that the typical lack of risk diversification in "small" firms might provide a case for offering income insurance to such firms by taxing their income at a higher marginal (but not at a higher average) rate than the tax rate applied to the income of large open corporations.

Admittedly, however, these arguments were rather speculative and therefore do not provide a very strong case for a significant and systematic tax differentiation between small and large firms. In particular, we are not in a position to offer even a rough quantitative estimate of the optimal degree of tax differentiation across the different organizational forms.

Furthermore, experience suggests that once policymakers attempt to differentiate tax rates on different forms of economic activity, the tax system tends to become more vulnerable to special interest groups pressing for all sorts of tax privileges. Given our present state of knowledge, policymakers may therefore be well advised to stick to the conventional norm of tax neutrality, implying that physical assets should be taxed according to roughly the same rules – regardless of the type of organization in which they are invested, and that human capital should be taxed in roughly the same way – whether it is employed in the owner's own firm or in the market for hired labor. At the same time, however, our analysis of risk issues suggests that a tax system that at the margin imposes some degree of tax progressivity on the income of small firms cannot *a priori* be considered to be distortionary and discriminatory, even if income from large corporations is taxed at a relatively low proportional rate.

In fact, the very notion of neutrality becomes more complicated in the presence of risk. A tax system is commonly said to be neutral if it merely generates income effects, i.e. if it does not distort the taxpayer's incentives for choosing between competing alternatives. Under full certainty, neutrality is achieved by taxing all physical assets according to the same rules and tax rates and irrespective of how the firm is organized. However, under uncertainty an income tax does not only tax away income; it also implies redistribution of risks. Thus, as shown in the appendix, taxing returns from risky assets at the same effective tax rate may affect their after-tax ranking. Hence, what is commonly called a "neutral" tax system may in fact distort the allocation of resources. When all types of assets and incomes are taxed according to the same rules and tax schedules, it would perhaps be more appropriate to speak of a "symmetric" tax system, hence reserving the term "neutrality" for the theoretical ideal of a tax system without distortionary effects. However, below we shall adhere to conventional terminology and refer to a tax system that treats different investors, assets, firms and incomes symmetrically as a 'neutral' system.

Parts III and IV will discuss the practical problems of taxing the self-employed, given that policymakers wish to achieve some rough degree of tax neutrality (symmetry).

III. TAXATION OF THE SELF-EMPLOYED: ALTERNATIVE METHODS OF INCOME SPLITTING

III.1. The motivation for splitting the income of the self-employed

We noted in the introduction that a neutral tax treatment of the self-employed would automatically be achieved under a global comprehensive income tax, which would subject the sum of the taxpayer's incomes from all sources to a single personal tax schedule. Under such a truly comprehensive income tax, both retained and distributed corporate profits would be attributed to individual shareholders and would be taxed according to the same personal tax schedule as would profits from unincorporated firms.

However, in practice no country has yet attempted to tax all retained corporate profits at the shareholder level, since this might involve liquidity problems for shareholders, and since it would entail serious administrative problems, owing to the fact that shares in individual corporations are often traded several times within the fiscal year. Moreover, as described in Sørensen (1994), several good reasons exist to explain why income from capital should not be taxed at the same (marginal) rate as income from labor, and the Nordic countries have in fact introduced separate taxation of the two types of income.

Under these circumstances, a neutral tax treatment of income from self-employment *vis á vis* wage income and corporate source income will require a splitting of taxable income from self-employment into different components which are (roughly) comparable to these other types of income.

III.2. Alternative methods of income splitting: The "Fence model" versus the "Source model"

During the last two decades, Nordic tax policymakers have focused on two alternative methods of income splitting for the self-employed:

The so-called "Fence model" (henceforth termed the F-model) aims at separating the income retained for accumulation in the firm from the income withdrawn from the firm for private consumption or savings purposes of the owner. In other words, the F-model divides the income and wealth of the self-employed into a "business sphere" and a "private sphere," establishing a "fence" between the two spheres.[25]

The second method of income splitting is the so-called "Source model" (S-model), which aims at splitting up the total income of the self-employed into an estimated income from capital and an estimated income from labor.

The purpose of the F-model has typically been seen as that of allowing income retained in unincorporated firms to be taxed at concessionary rates -- e.g. at the corporate income tax rate in cases where this rate falls short of the marginal personal income tax rate – while income withdrawn from the firm would be added to the possible other incomes of the owner and taxed at the ordinary personal tax rate. Sometimes the F-model has also been seen as a means of allowing full deductibility of interest on "business" debt, in circumstances where policymakers desired to restrict the deductibility of interest on "private" debt.

---

25. In Sweden this model is usually referred to as "staket-modellen," while the Norwegian Aarbakke Committee used the term "uttaks-modellen."

By contrast, the S-model was developed primarily to ensure an equitable tax treatment of the self-employed relative to wage earners and recipients of income from "passive" investments under a tax system which systematically differentiates the tax rates on labor income and on capital income.

In practice, it is possible to combine elements of the F-model and the S-model, as is done in the Danish and the Swedish tax schemes for the self-employed, which will be described later.

III.3. Some problems with the "Fence model"

Perhaps the most obvious problem relating to the F-model is that of dividing the assets and liabilities of the self-employed into a "private" sphere and a "business" sphere. If the return to savings undertaken within the business is taxed at a lower rate than the return to "private" savings invested outside the business sphere, the taxpayer will have an incentive to register "private" assets as business assets. The reason is that even though a surtax equal to the difference between the tax rate on retained earnings and the marginal personal income tax rate will be levied when the savings are ultimately withdrawn from the business, the proprietor will still gain from being able to accumulate earnings at the low business tax rate rather than having to pay ordinary personal income tax on the return to savings during the entire accumulation period. In short, there is a tax credit gain from the deferral of the surtax.

As a parallel, if full deductibility of interest on "business" debt is combined with restrictions on the deductibility of interest on "private" debt, the self-employed will have an incentive to register private debt as business debt. Since no objectively correct dividing line exists between the two categories of debt, it will inevitably be difficult for the tax authorities to prove that a given liability should not be registered as business debt – at least as long as the registered net equity of the business is positive. Consequently, the introduction of an F-model, with the purpose of restricting or eliminating the deductibility of interest on private debt, will tend to be equivalent to a scheme that restricts or eliminates interest deductibility for wage earners while retaining (close to) full deductibility for the self-employed.

Even if the practical problems of dividing the assets and liabilities of the self-employed could be overcome, an F-model offering low rates of tax on retained business profits would still create a number of economic distortions. The model would obviously make it more attractive to retain profits within the business rather than withdrawing them for the purpose of investment in the capital market. In this way the F-model could promote retentions-financed investment in the unincorporated sector at the expense of other investments with a higher social (pre-tax) rate of return.

To illustrate, suppose that profits retained in the business are taxed at a rate equal to the corporate tax rate τ, while capital income from other sources is taxed at the marginal personal rate t. Furthermore, suppose, as a first approximation, that taxable business profits correspond to true economic profits. For a self-employed taxpayer, the required pre-tax rate of return c on retentions-financed investment in the firm will then be given by the arbitrage condition

$$c(1-\tau) = i(1-t) \tag{1}$$

where i is the market rate of interest before tax. This condition simply says that the marginal after-tax return on investment within the firm must equal the net rate of return that might be earned in the capital market.[26] By comparison, the required rate of return on retentions-financed investment undertaken by a *corporation* will be given by

$$c(1-\tau)(1-z) = i(1-t) \tag{2}$$

where z is the effective personal tax rate on accrued capital gains on shares.[27] This equation states that the net return available to shareholders after payment of corporate and personal tax must be at least as high as the after-tax interest income that they might have earned by investing in bonds rather than shares. Comparing the two arbitrage conditions, we

26. Notice that the surtax that is due when the retained profits are ultimately taken out of the firm has no affect on the required rate of return on retentions-financed investment. The reason is that this surtax on distributed profits reduces the opportunity cost of retained earnings by the same proportion as it reduces the net income, which will ultimately be at the owner's disposal when profits are paid out.

27. By analogy to the previous arbitrage condition, the personal tax rate on dividends does not affect the required return on retentions-financed corporate investment because the dividend tax reduces the opportunity cost of retained corporate profits to the same extent as it reduces the net income available to shareholders when profits are ultimately paid out.

see that – to the extent that shareholders are taxed on the capital gains on shares resulting from retentions – the required pre-tax rate of return on corporate investment financed by retained profits will *ceteris paribus* exceed the required return on corresponding investment undertaken in the non-corporate sector.

The F-model would also provide an incentive for the self-employed to shift private consumption activities to the business sphere, where consumed income is taxed at a lower rate. Generally, the F-model would thus tend to produce a "lock-in" effect by stimulating consumption as well as investment within unincorporated firms at the expense of consumption and investment outside that sector.

It might be argued that the alleged locking-in of resources in the non-corporate sector serves mainly to offset a similar locking-in of resources in the corporate sector stemming from the combination of a relatively low corporate tax rate and a lenient taxation of capital gains on shares. Referring back to the discussion in section II.3, one might also argue that a favorable tax treatment of the retained profits of small firms may be justified if the private cost of equity capital for such firms exceeds the social cost, owing to the fact that the owners of small firms do not have the opportunity to diversify all of their socially diversifiable risks.

Furthermore, many policymakers seem to believe that liberal tax treatment of the retained earnings of the self-employed can be justified by the fact that the expansion of small firms is hampered by more severe credit constraints than those faced by large firms. One might hypothesize that the problems of asymmetric information giving rise to credit rationing are more serious in small private firms than they are in large open corporations – which are subject to more systematic external monitoring, due to government regulations and the incentives of the stock market. On the other hand, the management problems of large corporations are often considerably more complex than those facing small firms, so it is not obvious that asymmetric information is in fact a greater problem in the latter category of firms. Moreover, it is a moot point whether credit constraints arising from asymmetric information do in fact lead to a suboptimal level of investment. In the well-known model of credit rationing developed by Stiglitz and Weiss (1981), where all agents are assumed to be risk neutral, the level of investment is indeed below the social optimum, because some investments with an expected return above the rate of interest on safe assets are not undertaken, as De Meza and Webb (1987) demonstrated. However, in the models set up by Keeton (1979) and Williamson (1986) the credit-rationed market equilibrium is in fact socially optimal, provided the government has no more information on investment projects than do private lenders. In these models credit rationing is an efficient method of preventing over-investment that would otherwise take place because of the lender's lack of information.

Despite the merits of the arguments for a favorable tax treatment of the returns to physical investment retained by the self-employed, the F-model still fails to ensure a neutral tax treatment of the self-employed *vis á vis wage earners.* The reason is that the F-model enables the self-employed to postpone the progressive surtaxes on *labor* income retained in the firm, thereby obtaining a liquidity gain from tax deferral, which is not available to wage earners.

We thus conclude that the F-model is not well suited to satisfy the goal of tax neutrality. Below we shall therefore focus on the problems of designing a "Source-model" of business income taxation that involves no systematic bias in favor of or against income from self-employment under a "dual" income tax system of the Nordic type (with different personal tax rates on income from labor and income from capital).

IV. ISSUES OF BUSINESS TAX DESIGN UNDER A DUAL INCOME TAX

IV.1 Imputation of labor income versus imputation of capital income

In the pure version of the Nordic system of dual income taxation, income from capital is taxed at a flat rate equal to the corporate income tax rate, while income from labor and from other sources is taxed according to a progressive tax schedule. The purpose of the "Source model" of business income taxation is to split income from self-employment into a labor income component and a capital income component to obtain at least a rough tax neutrality between wage earners and the self-employed. To the extent that corporate profits represent a return to capital, the S-model will also ensure rough tax neutrality between corporate source income and income from self-employment, since the return to the capital invested by the self-employed will be taxed at a capital income tax rate equal to the corporate income tax rate.

The splitting of income from self-employment could be implemented by imputing wage income to the owner-manager and categorizing the remaining business income as capital income. Alternatively, one could impute a return to the capital invested in the firm and categorize the residual business income as labor income.

These two procedures for income splitting obviously have different implications for the marginal tax rate faced by the self-employed. Roughly speaking, the Nordic countries tax labor income according to a progressive rate schedule, while they tax capital income at a flat rate equal to the lower rate in the labor income tax schedule.[28] If the capital income of the self-employed were to be calculated as a residual after deduction of a fixed imputed wage rate, the marginal tax rate of the self-employed would equal the low tax rate on capital income. The average tax rate imposed on the self-employed would thus fall with rising business incomes; that is, the system would tend to be regressive. Conversely, if labor income were to be calculated as the residual after deduction of an imputed return to business assets, an increase in business income would be taxed according to the progressive schedule applied to labor income.

Since regressivity of the business income tax seems to be inconsistent with the goal of vertical taxpayer equity and with the desire for macroeconomic stabilization, it would appear that the categorization of residual business income as progressively taxed labor income would be the more attractive alternative from the perspective of equity and stabilization. Administrative considerations tend to strengthen this conclusion, since in practice it would be very difficult for the authorities to estimate a proper imputed wage income for the self-employed, given that work efforts and individual talents differ, and given that market wages for similar types of labor often differ substantially.

In addition, our previous analysis of risk issues suggests an efficiency case for progressive taxation of the residual income of the self-employed, since a relatively high marginal tax rate offers a high degree of income insurance. With progressive taxation of residual income, the actual taxation of realized returns on physical investment will also be progressive, with the effective marginal tax rate equal to the flat

28. In Denmark, there is some amount of progressivity in the taxation of capital income, as explained in Sørensen (1994).

statutory rate on capital income only if the realized rate of return happens to equal the imputed one. If the realized rate of return is higher than the imputed rate, the effective marginal tax rate will tend to be higher than the flat tax rate on capital income, while the opposite will hold if the realized return falls short of the imputed return, since the difference between these two rates of return will then be deductible against taxable labor income, thereby partly or fully offsetting the tax liability on imputed capital income. Obviously, such tax rules subsidize the less profitable and penalize the more profitable investment projects, as compared with investments undertaken by corporate firms, which are not subject to the splitting of business income. However, given the limited possibilities for proprietors to diversify their risks, such tax differentiation may in fact be efficient, as we argued in section II.3.

IV.2 Assessing the value of business assets

To estimate the capital income of the self-employed by imputing a return to their business assets, the tax authorities must define these assets and the valuation rules to be applied in assessing their value for tax purposes.

From an administrative viewpoint it is natural to include depreciable business assets at the value assessed for purposes of the income and/or wealth tax, even if this would imply some undervaluation in circumstances where accelerated depreciation is allowed. Indeed, this procedure could serve to counteract the distortionary reduction of the cost of capital caused by accelerated depreciation, since such "excessive" depreciation would reduce the imputed return to capital, thereby increasing the share of business income that is taxed according to the progressive labor-income tax schedule. For assets used for private as well as business purposes (e.g. cars), special registration and valuation procedures must be designed.

A special problem relates to the valuation of intangible assets such as goodwill, patents, know-how, organizational "infrastructure" and special managerial skills. If investment in such assets cannot be expensed immediately, the value of these investments clearly ought to be included in the registered business assets which serve as a basis for calculating the imputed capital income of the proprietor. Otherwise, the return to intangible assets would be subject to the progressive labor income tax and would hence be overtaxed relative to the return to physical assets.

However, many types of investment in intangible assets can in fact be expensed immediately and are thus taxed on a cash-flow basis,[29] implying a zero effective marginal tax rate on the return to these investments (provided the proprietor's marginal tax rate at the time of investment equals his marginal tax rate when the cash return flows in). Thus, it is quite conceivable that the return to some intangibles could be undertaxed relative to the profits from physical assets, even if intangibles are not included in the basis for calculating the imputed rate of return.

In practice, problems of valuation will probably prevent many types of intangibles from being registered as business assets.

IV.3 The treatment of financial assets and liabilities: The "gross" method versus the "net" method

Another question is whether the financial assets and liabilities of the business should be included in the basis for calculating the imputed rate of return. In this context, a choice must be made between the following two alternative procedures:

Under the so-called "gross" method, the net financial liabilities of the firm are not deducted from the asset base. Thus, the labor income of the proprietor is calculated by deducting an imputed return to "gross" business assets from the "gross" profits of the firm (defined as profits *before* interest), and net capital income is calculated by deducting interest expenses from the imputed return to the gross assets.

By contrast, capital income is calculated under the "net" method by imputing a return to the net assets of the firm (business assets minus business debt), and labor income is found by deducting this imputed return to net equity from net profits (defined as profits *after* deduction for interest).

If the imputed rate of return equals the rate of interest paid (or earned) by the proprietor, the gross and net methods will be equivalent. This point is illustrated by the simplified numerical example in Table 1, which shows that the estimated income from capital and labor is exactly the same under the two methods, given that the percentage imputed

29. This is true, for instance, for most advertisement expenses, serving to build up goodwill. Usually, the costs of research and development are also immediately deductible.

rate of return corresponds to the interest rate paid on business debt (assumed here to be 10%).

However, this equivalence breaks down when the interest rate actually paid (or earned) by the proprietor deviates from the imputed rate of return. Thus, if the imputed percentage rate of return exceeds the interest rate, the gross method will impute a higher capital income and a correspondingly lower labor income to the proprietor, compared to the net method. For instance, if the imputed rate of return in the example in table 1 was 15% instead of 10%, the estimated capital income under the gross method would rise to 70,000 kroner, while the estimated labor income would fall to 150,000 kroner; the net method, conversely, would impute a capital income of 30,000 kroner and a labor income of 190,000 kroner to the proprietor. Given that labor income is taxed at a higher marginal rate than is capital income, the gross method would then obviously be more favorable to the self-employed in this case than would the net method. Yet, it is easy to verify that the opposite would be true if the percentage imputed rate of return falls short of the market interest rate on business debt.

When the imputed rate of return deviates from the market interest rate, the gross method has the disadvantage of distorting investment incentives. For instance, suppose a businessman faces a borrowing rate of interest of 15%. In the absence of tax he would then wish to carry debt-financed investment to the point where the (risk-adjusted) rate of return on the marginal investment project is just equal to 15%. Suppose now that taxation under the gross method only imputes a return of, say, 10% to business assets. In that case, one third of the return on the marginal investment project just mentioned would be categorized as labor income and subjected to progressive taxation, whereas the entire 15% interest on the loan would be deductible only against the (low) flat tax rate on capital income. Consequently, the project would carry a positive tax burden and would no longer be profitable. On the other hand, if the rate of return imputed to business assets were higher than the businessman's marginal borrowing rate of interest, the tax system would artificially encourage investment. In a similar vein, it may easily be demonstrated that the gross method would tend to distort equity-financed investment if the rate of imputation for tax purposes deviates from the proprietor's opportunity cost of capital (e.g. the rate of return he could obtain on passive investment in the capital market).

These investment distortions are, in principle, avoided under the net method, which imputes a return not only to non-financial business assets, but also to the proprietor's net financial assets. In that case a debt-financed investment or an investment financed by a reduction in the financial assets of the entrepreneur would not change the registered net assets of the business and the imputed return to these assets. The earnings from the extra investment would thus be subject to the marginal tax rate applicable to labor income, but the financial cost of the investment would be deductible against the same marginal tax rate; it would thus always pay the entrepreneur to carry investment to the point where its marginal return before tax is just equal to the financial (opportunity) cost before tax.[30]

To guarantee investment neutrality, it would thus seem desirable to deduct net financial business liabilities from the base for the calculation of the imputed return and to allow deduction for net interest payments from taxable business income, as done under the "net" method.

Unfortunately, however, this would also leave the self-employed with certain arbitrage opportunities. More specifically, in cases where the interest rate on "private" (i.e. non-business) debt exceeds the rate of return imputed to business equity, proprietors would be able to reduce their total tax liability by registering their private debt as business debt. For instance, suppose the interest rate on private debt is 20%, whereas the imputed return is only 10%. An entrepreneur transferring a debt of 100,000 kroner from the private sphere to the business sphere would then register a fall in taxable business income of 20,000 kroner – due to increased "business" interest payments. Half of this amount (0.1x100,000) would be categorized as a fall in the capital income attributed to the business, while the remaining 10,000 kroner would be registered as a fall in labor income. If the marginal tax rate on labor income is 60% and the tax rate on capital income is 30%, the total fall in taxes on income deriving from the business would thus be 10,000 x 0.6 + 10,000 x 0.3 = 9,000 kroner. In the "private" sphere, the entrepreneur would of course no longer be able to deduct the interest of 20,000 kroner from his capital income, so the tax bill on income from this sphere would increase by

30. Strictly speaking, the "net" method will be fully neutral towards debt-financed investment only when depreciation for tax purposes corresponds to true economic depreciation. At the present stage, we wish only to point out that the net method has a "neutrality advantage" over the gross method, provided that business profits are measured "correctly."

20,000 x 0.3 = 6,000 kroner. After all this, the businessman would still be left with a net gain in disposable income of 9,000-6,000 = 3,000 kroner.

The scope for tax avoidance through such transfers of debt to the business sphere could be even greater if the entrepreneur has already transferred so much private debt to the business that the registered net equity of the firm is zero. In the example just considered, the further transfer of 100,000 kroner of private debt to the business will then still reduce taxable business profits by the interest payment of 20,000 kroner, but there will be no reduction in the imputed capital income deriving from the business, since this imputed return has already been brought down to zero. Hence, the effect of the transaction will be to reduce the estimated labor income from the business by 20,000 kroner, implying a fall of 0.6 x 20,000 = 12,000 kroner in the labor income tax liability, and to increase net capital income from "private" sources by 20,000 kroner, leading to an increased capital income tax liability of 0.3 x 20,000 = 6,000 kroner. Obviously, the net tax saving will then amount to 6,000 kroner.

To limit the gain from this sort of tax arbitrage, it is natural to adjust business income by an imputed interest income in cases where the registered net equity of the firm is negative, since such negative equity may be taken as evidence that private (non-business) liabilities have improperly been transferred to the business. If we stick to the example above -- where the initial net equity is zero and the entrepreneur transfers an additional debt of 200,000 kroner to his business – an imputed interest on the resulting negative net equity of 200,000 kroner would then be added back to recorded business income (to offset the effect of increased interest deductions from business profits), and a corresponding imputed interest income would be deducted from the businessman's registered net capital income from the "private" sphere. However, while such an "interest correction" would clearly serve to reduce the taxpayer's net gain from transfers of private debt to the business sphere, it would fail to neutralize the gain completely as long as the imputed rate of interest falls short of the actual interest rate paid on private debt. Thus, if the imputed interest rate is only 10%, while the actual interest rate is 20%, the entrepreneur in the example above would still make a net gain of 3,000 kroner by transferring private debt to the business.

Under the net method, an "interest correction" may also be called for in other cases. For example, suppose the imputed return in any year is calculated on the basis of registered net business equity on December 31 of the previous year. On January 1, the entrepreneur may then withdraw funds from the business and invest them in the capital market at the going market interest rate, and reinject the funds back into the business on December 31 of the same year. This transaction will leave the registered net business equity and hence the imputed return unaffected, but it will clearly reduce business profits after interest – by increasing the net financial liabilities of the firm between January 1 and December 31 – and will thus reduce the residual business income subject to the marginal labor-income tax rate. On the other hand, the registered "private" capital income of the proprietor will go up by a similar amount – due to the interest income earned on the financial investment in the capital market – but this income will be taxed at the low rate applying to capital income. In this way does the proprietor succeed in converting highly taxed labor income (residual business income) into lightly taxed capital income. To offset the gains from such transactions, tax authorities may find it necessary to undertake an "interest correction" – adding an imputed interest income to recorded business profits and deducting a similar amount from recorded capital income – in cases where the proprietor withdraws funds from the firm only to reinject them later in the same fiscal year. Again, such an attempt to discourage tax arbitrage would work perfectly only if the imputed interest income equals the actual interest rate earned by the businessman.

To elaborate further on tax arbitrage opportunities under the net method, examine the cases in which the imputed rate of return exceeds the actual rate of interest on business debt. In these circumstances, the self-employed will be able to reduce their total tax liability by transferring such debt to the private sphere, since this would imply a transformation of labor income (residual business income) into capital income.

By contrast, under the "gross" method, which renders financial liabilities non-deductible from the base for the calculation of the imputed return, and which allows all interest payments ("business" as well as "private" interest) to be deductible only against the tax rate for capital income, the tax arbitrage just described would not be possible.

The choice between the "gross" method and the "net" method of splitting the income of the self-employed seems thus to involve a trade-off between the goal of investment neutrality (implying a preference for the net method) and the desire to minimize administrative complexity and the scope for tax arbitrage (which clearly implies a preference for the gross method).

However, whether or not "business" debt and the associated interest payments are deductible from the net assets and the net income of the business, respectively, an incentive will always exist for entrepreneurs to register "private" assets with a yield below the imputed rate of return as business assets, since they can thereby reduce the proportion of their total income that will be subject to the high marginal tax rate on labor income. For example, if a "private" piece of land or real estate yielding no current rental income could be categorized as a business asset, total taxable business income would be unaffected (abstracting from a possible capital gains tax liability), but a greater part of this income would be treated as lightly taxed capital income imputed to "business" assets.

The scope for such tax-minimizing asset transactions can of course be reduced by the authorities carefully defining the type of assets that can be categorized as business assets, but the activity probably cannot be fully eliminated. These observations suggest that any version of the S-model is likely to leave the self-employed with at least some maneuvering room for reducing their tax liability through an appropriate categorization of their assets and liabilities.

It is only fair to add that the S-model may also sometimes imply a rather heavy tax burden for the self-employed. For instance, this may be the case under the gross method in circumstances where unfavorable market developments have reduced the value of business assets to such an extent that the base for calculating the imputed return to these assets falls short of the stock of business debt. The entrepreneur will then record a negative net capital income, which may be deducted only against the low tax rate on such income (whereas all of his gross business profits will be taxed progressively as labor income). A similar situation may arise under the net method, if the "interest correction" described above is applied in all circumstances in which the net equity of the business turns negative.

Furthermore, if valuation problems prevent intangible assets from being included in the asset base for calculating the imputed return, the self-employed may end up being taxed too heavily if the costs of acquiring the intangibles cannot be expensed or capitalized and written off against taxable profits. Again, the problem is that the returns to these assets end up being taxed progressively as labor income.

IV.4 Choosing the imputed rate of return

The analysis above indicates that the magnitude of the rate of return imputed to business assets will be crucial for the extent and character of the tax arbitrage opportunities of the self-employed. As we have seen, it will also be decisive for the neutrality properties (or lack thereof) of the business income tax, particularly under the so-called "gross" method of splitting the income of the self-employed. If the imputed rate of return is set at a low level, this will tend to discourage investment in unincorporated firms relative to the no-tax situation, whereas such investment will tend to be "artificially" stimulated if the rate of return is set at a high level.

One issue to be resolved is whether the imputed return should take the form of a nominal or a real rate of return? The answer seems fairly straightforward: if the assessed value of business assets is not indexed for inflation (being instead based on historical acquisition prices minus accumulated depreciation allowances), it would be logical to apply a nominal rate of return covering the real return as well as an inflation premium. On the other hand, if book values for tax purposes are indexed in accordance with inflation, it would be natural to impute only a real return to the indexed asset values.

The choice of a proper level of the imputed rate of return – be it a nominal or a real return – also involves more fundamental problems. The analysis from the previous section suggests that the imputed return should correspond to the rate of interest on the assets and liabilities of the self-employed. However, in practice there is rarely such a thing as "the" going market rate of interest which could serve as a natural standard for setting the imputed rate of return. At the very least the self-employed (like other investors) are usually faced with a difference between the rate of interest at which they can borrow, and the interest rate they can earn on bank deposits and other passive financial investments. The (opportunity) cost of finance will thus vary according to how the entrepreneur finances investment: by borrowing or by selling off financial assets. If the authorities wish to set the imputed rate of return at a level that would be neutral towards business investment decisions, it is thus important for them to know whether marginal investments are typically financed by debt or by equity. No general answer can probably be given to this question.

Another problem is that the imputed return ought to include a risk premium in order to avoid discouraging active business investment relative to passive financial investment in safe assets. To ensure neutrality, this risk premium should, ideally, vary with the risk characteristics of each individual investment project or at least be differentiated across the different sectors of the economy according to differences in non-diversifiable risks. However, the tax authorities lack the information and the administrative capabilities needed to undertake such a detailed and rational differentiation of risk premia. Therefore, imputed risk premia will inevitably be too high for some investment projects and too low for other projects, thereby introducing new sources of investment distortions in addition to those stemming from deviations from true economic depreciation, etc..

V. THE TAXATION OF THE SELF-EMPLOYED IN THE NORDIC COUNTRIES

V.1 Background and notation

We shall now briefly describe how the four major Nordic countries have dealt with the problems (see Parts III & IV) of taxing the self-employed.

In recent years the Nordic countries have abandoned the principle of global income taxation in favor of a system of "dual" income taxation, according to which capital income is taxed at a flat rate (approximately) equal to the corporate income tax rate, whereas the taxpayer's total income from other sources – which is termed "personal income" or "earned income" – is taxed according to a progressive tax schedule. As explained in Sørensen (1994), the introduction of this new tax system has been motivated *inter alia* by desires to reduce the distortionary effects of progressive income taxation in an inflationary environment, to strengthen private savings incentives, to limit the scope for tax arbitrage, and to eliminate the revenue losses stemming from deductibility of nominal interest expenses against the high top marginal income tax rates.

In the early 1990s, Finland, Norway and Sweden all introduced rather "pure" versions of the dual income tax. Denmark implemented a variant of the dual income tax as early as 1987, but the recent 1994

Danish tax reform introduces new elements of progressivity in the taxation of capital income. However, the 1994 Danish tax reform also introduces new social security taxes that are levied only on earned income, so the effective marginal tax rate on such income remains above the top marginal tax rate on capital income.

The tax code in all four countries requires a splitting of taxable income from self-employment into a capital income component and a "personal" ("earned") income component in accordance with the "Source model." Norway has chosen to split the income of the self-employed according to the "gross" method described in section IV.3, while Denmark, Finland and Sweden have implemented variants of the "net" method of income splitting. As we shall see, Denmark and Sweden have also introduced elements of the "Fence model" (sketched in Part III) into their tax code for the self-employed.

We will use the following notation to summarize the tax rules for proprietors in the four countries:

A = book value of business assets in the tax accounts

B = stock of business debt

T = total tax liability on business income

Y = business profits before interest ("gross" profits)

i = nominal rate of interest

k = imputed (nominal) rate of return on business assets

t = tax rate on capital income

m = effective tax rate on personal (earned) income of the self-employed

τ = tax rate on profits retained in the business

The effective tax rate on earned business income consists of the sum of the personal income tax rate (m^p) and the social security tax rate (s^s) levied on the earned income of the self-employed. In Denmark and Sweden the social security tax is deductible from the base of the personal income tax; for these countries, thus, we have

$$m = s^s + m^p (1 - s^s) \tag{3}$$

As long as we focus on the proprietor's *total* tax bill, tax rates t and m should be interpreted as *average* tax rates. Since earned income is subject to progressive taxation, the average tax rate on such income will be a weighted average of the marginal tax rates in the different brackets of the tax schedule.

The next four sections state the main principles for taxation of income from self-employment in the Nordic countries after the recent tax reforms.[31] Note that we neglect a number of temporary transition rules embodied in the reforms, since we aim to illustrate the rules that will prevail when the new tax systems have been fully phased in. First are Norway and Finland, where the basic taxation principles are simpler than they are in Denmark and Sweden. Since Part II argued that the organizational form of the closed corporation is a close substitute for the proprietorship form, we shall also briefly sketch the main rules in each of the four countries for taxing closed corporations with active owners. We describe only the general principles for calculating the tax liability, without indicating the specific tax rates applied in the four countries.

V.2 Norway

Norway is the only Nordic country that has chosen to split the income of proprietors by means of the "gross" method, whereby an imputed return on gross business assets is taxed as capital income and is deducted from business profits before interest to arrive at the proprietor's estimated earned income. This equation follows for the tax bill for a Norwegian proprietor:

$$T = t\,(kA - iB) + m\,(Y - kA) \qquad (4)$$

The first term on the right-hand side of (4) is the capital income tax, which is levied on the imputed return to business assets minus the interest expenses of the proprietor. The second term represents the tax on the estimated personal income, with the latter being equal to gross business profits (that is, profits before interest), minus the imputed return to gross business assets.

The imputed rate of return is set equal to the market interest rate on five-year government bonds plus a risk premium of six percentage

31. The tax rules referred to are those which applied in 1994.

points. The business assets to which this rate of return is imputed include physical business assets, acquired (but not self-created) goodwill and other acquired intangibles, business inventories, and credit extended to customers net of debt to the firm's suppliers.

Two modifications exist to the tax rules sketched in (4), which should be mentioned here: First, if the estimated personal income of the proprietor exceeds 1.25 million Norwegian kroner (1993-level), the excess amount is in fact taxed as capital income. The motivation for this rule is that if residual profits are very high relative to a "normal" wage income, part of these profits is likely to represent a return to capital rather than a reward for labor. Accordingly, the tax schedule for proprietors with very high incomes is in fact regressive, with a marginal tax rate equal to the flat rate of tax on capital income.

The second modification is that proprietors who have employees are allowed to make a so-called "salary deduction" amounting to 12% of their wage bill from taxable personal (earned) income, subject to the constraint that the estimated personal income of the employer cannot fall below 145% of the salary of the highest paid employee. The official rationale for the "salary deduction" is that the personal income for owners of firms with little investment and many employees would otherwise be unreasonably high, and that the deduction should compensate for the fact that self-created goodwill is not included in the basis for calculating the imputed rate of return.

The above tax rules for proprietorships and partnerships also apply to income from *corporations,* where at least two thirds of the shares are owned by "active" shareholders, that is, those who invest a certain personal effort in the company's business. The limit for "activity" is set at a rather low level. To prevent the two-thirds rule from being circumvented by transfers of shares to spouses, relatives and controlled companies, the authorities have established intricate identification rules. These rules appear to have stimulated considerable tax planning activity.

The tax rules for corporations with active owners imply that the residual profits of these companies are taxed as personal (earned) income of the owners – even if the profits are not actually distributed. In these cases the owners may claim a refund from the company for the taxes on retained profits attributed to them as personal income.

V.3 Finland

As part of its ambitious 1993 reform of capital income taxation, Finland introduced a pure version of the "net" method, which calculates the capital income of the self-employed as an imputed rate of return on the book value of the *net* assets of the business, and which estimates the earned income of the proprietor as net business profits (profits net of interest) minus the imputed return on net assets. Hence the tax bill of the proprietor is given as

$$T = tk\,(A - B\ ) + m\,[Y - iB - k\,(A - B\ ) \qquad (5)$$

For the time being, the imputed rate of return on net business assets has been set at 15%. Proprietors with employees are allowed to make a deduction of up to 10% of their wage bill from their taxable earned income.

The tax rules for proprietors and partnerships summarized in equation (5) are also applied to *all* corporations that are not listed in the Helsinki stock exchange or in a foreign stock exchange. By adopting this rather radical provision, Finnish tax law has cut through the problems of defining categories such as "active" shareholders or closely held companies.

V.4 Denmark

The Danish introduced their business tax scheme for the self-employed simultaneously with the dual income tax in 1987. The scheme represents a rather complicated mixture of the "Source model" and the "Fence model" described in parts III and IV.

The principles of the scheme may be explained as follows: First, a return is imputed to the *net* assets of the business. The return is imputed at a rate equal to the average market interest rate on bonds during the first half of the year, and it is taxed as capital income. Second, the imputed return is deducted from net taxable profits (profits net of interest) in order to arrive at "residual profits." The part of residual profits that is distributed to the owner is taxed as personal (earned) income, whereas the part that is retained in the business is subject to a preliminary flat tax, which is levied at a rate equal to the corporate income tax rate. If retained profits are distributed later, they are added to the proprietor's personal income and taxed as such, with the previous preliminary tax being deducted from the final tax bill to avoid double taxation. Thus, the preliminary tax serves as a withholding tax on retained profits, which are later distributed. At the same time, the preliminary tax enables proprietorships to accumulate income within the business on the same tax terms as corporations.

If E is the accumulated stock of retained profits before tax, and E with a dot superscript is the rate of change of E over the fiscal year (i.e. current retentions), we may summarize the Danish business tax scheme for the self-employed in the following equation:

$$T = tk\,(A - B\,) + \tau\dot{E} + m\,[\,Y - iB - k\,(A - B\,) - \dot{E}\,] \tag{6}$$

From the explanation above it follows that equation (6) is valid whether current retentions are positive (in which case part of residual profits are being retained in the business) or negative (in which case previous retentions are being distributed).

In principle, equation (6) also holds if the registered net assets of the business *(A - B)* turn negative. Such a negative balance is considered to be evidence that the proprietor has transferred "private" debt to the business sphere, or that he has incurred "private" debt by letting the firm borrow on his behalf. In that case a so-called "interest correction" of the kind explained in section IV.3 is made; that is, an imputed interest on the negative net business assets is added to taxable business income and subtracted from the proprietor's net capital income to adjust for the fact that the proprietor has imposed "private" interest expenses on his business. This procedure ensures that interest on "private" debt cannot be deducted against the top marginal tax rate on personal income. However, the proprietor may avoid such an "interest correction" if he can verify that all of the liabilities registered in the business do in fact represent legitimate business debt. In that case, the registered net assets of the firm are set equal to zero, and the proprietor's tax bill equals

$$T = \tau\dot{E} + m\,(\,Y - iB - \dot{E}\,) \tag{7}$$

Danish proprietors may also choose to be taxed according to a simplified scheme ("kapitalafkastmodellen") that splits their income into a capital income component and a personal income component in accordance with the "gross" method also applied in Norway. The tax bill will then be given by an expression identical to equation (4). Because it is much simpler, thereby involving lower compliance costs than the business tax scheme described above, taxation according to this "gross" method may be attractive for proprietors who are unable or unwilling to accumulate profits within the firm.

Danish tax law does *not* apply the tax rules for the self-employed to the owners of closely held corporations with active owners. These corporations are simply taxed according to the general rules applying to all other corporations. Since active owners of closely held corporations may to a large extent determine whether their income from the corporation should take the form of (management) salaries, of dividends, or of capital gains on shares, these taxpayers may have ample room for reducing their tax burden if the marginal tax rates on these three forms of income differ from each other. However, Danish authorities more or less avoided this problem because the tax code implies a certain amount of double taxation of income from stockholding. Thus, when the combined effect of the corporate income tax and the special (progressive) tax on "shareholder income" (dividends plus realized capital gains on shares) is taken into account, the resulting total corporate and personal marginal tax rate on corporate source income is very close to the top marginal tax rate on earned income, leaving no major gains to be reaped from transforming one form of income into another.[32]

V.5 Sweden

As of 1994, the Swedish government introduced a splitting of the income of the self-employed, as a follow-up on the tax reform of 1991, which introduced the dual income tax in Sweden. Like the Danish business tax scheme, the new Swedish tax rules for proprietors represent a hybrid between the "net" version of the "Source model" and a variant of the "Fence model." The new Swedish scheme thus allows residual profits

32. Of course, since the tax on capital gains on shares is deferred until the time of realization of the gain, the shareholder may still be able to gain from tax deferral if he is willing to postpone consumption of his income from the corporation.

retained in the business (so-called "expansionsmedel") to be taxed at a preliminary rate equal to the corporate tax rate, implying that only residual profits withdrawn from the firm are taxed as personal income.

However, the Swedish tax rules are less liberal than those of the Danes, since they do not allow so-called untaxed reserves to be included in the base for calculating the imputed rate of return. Recalling that E is our notation for the stock of accumulated retained earnings, then the untaxed reserves are defined as $E(1 - \tau)$, i.e., as that part of accumulated retentions that has not been paid in tax. On the other hand, the new Swedish tax law allows some income averaging through a deduction from taxable residual earnings for allocations to a "periodisation fund." More specifically, 25% of residual earnings may be set aside for the periodisation fund, but the amount allocated to the fund in any year must be added back into taxable residual earnings no later than five years after the allocation. Moreover, the amount set aside for the periodisation fund will be subtracted from the net equity base, which is used to calculate the imputed rate of return on business assets, causing a fall in imputed capital income and a corresponding rise in residual earnings. The periodisation fund, therefore, allows a deferral of the tax burden on only one quarter of residual earnings.

If P is the stock of reserves accumulated in the periodisation fund, and P with a dot superscript is the current addition (positive or negative) to these reserves, we may then specify the proprietor's tax bill under the new Swedish tax rules as follows:

$$T = tk\,[A - B - (1-\tau)E - P\,] + \tau\dot{E} + m^{e}\,(Y - iB - k\,\,[A - B - (1-\tau)E - P\,] - \dot{E} - \dot{P}\,) \qquad (8)$$

The imputed rate of return k is set equal to the interest rate on ten-year government bonds ("statslåneräntan") plus a premium of one percentage point. Like the Danish business tax scheme, the Swedish scheme requires an "interest correction" ("negativ räntefördelning") when the registered net assets of the business turn negative. Equation (8) therefore applies also when $A\text{-}B<0$.

Note that the proprietor is allowed to have his retentions taxed at the low corporate tax rate only as long as he does not violate the constraint

$$E\,(1-\tau) + P \leq A - B \qquad (9)$$

In other words, the sum of the accumulated amount of lightly taxed retentions and the untaxed reserves in the periodisation fund is not allowed to exceed the registered net equity of the firm.

The Swedish rules for taxation of partnerships ("handelsbolag"), corporations with a single owner ("enmansaktiebolag"), and corporations with a few "active" owners ("fåmansföretag") are similar to those applying to sole proprietors. Thus, an imputed return on a partner's ownership share of the firm's net assets is taxed as capital income, while his share of distributed residual profits is taxed as earned income. If residual profits are retained in the firm, they are taxed at the corporate tax rate.

In corporations with one or a few active owners, an imputed return on the acquisition price of the shares is treated as a dividend. If actual dividends exceed the imputed return, the difference is taxed as earned income of the shareholder. On the other hand, when the actual dividend is less than the imputed return, an amount equal to the difference may be taken out as a dividend in a later year. Until it is distributed, the amount is added to the basis for calculating the imputed return. Furthermore, if the sum of the shareholder's dividends and realized capital gains on shares in the company exceeds the imputed return, 70% of the residual gain is taxed as earned income, while the remaining 30% is taxed at the 12.5% capital gains tax rate. This highly schematic rule is intended to eliminate the possibilities for "active" shareholders to transform earned income into lightly taxed capital gains. To complicate matters further, there is an absolute limit to the amount of capital gain that may be taxed as earned income. Gains above the limit are taxed at the capital gains tax rate. Thus, there is element of regressivity in the tax schedule for capital gains on shares in closely held corporations.

VI. SUMMARY AND CONCLUSIONS

This paper has traveled a long route to study the theoretical and practical problems of taxing income from self-employment. In the Nordic countries, these problems have recently been accentuated by the switch to the system of "dual" income taxation, which taxes capital income at a low flat rate equal to the corporate income tax rate while subjecting earned income to a progressive tax schedule.

Adopting the criterion of economic efficiency, the paper started out discussing whether the return to the physical investment of proprietors should be taxed in the same way as the return to physical investment undertaken by corporations, and whether the returns to the human capital of the self-employed should be taxed in the same manner as the human capital of wage earners.

With regard to income from *physical* investment, we argued that it might be efficient to have a tax system which offers some income insurance to proprietors through a relatively high marginal tax rate - i.e., a marginal tax rate exceeding the corporate tax rate - because proprietors do not have the opportunities for risk diversification offered by the stock market and may therefore face a higher cost of equity capital than do large public corporations. At the same time, we noted that there seems to be no case for a higher *average* tax rate on proprietor income from physical investment.

In the same vein, we suggested that there might be an efficiency case for income insurance via a relatively high marginal tax rate combined with a moderate average tax rate on the return to the *human* capital of proprietors, since the self-employed do not have the same opportunities as wage earners to shift part of the risk associated with the employment of human capital onto an employer who may be in a better position to diversify the risk.

Thus, our analysis of risk issues indicated that a tax system that at the margin imposes some degree of tax progressivity on the income of small firms cannot *a priori* be regarded as distortionary and discriminatory. However, considering the speculative character of these arguments, and combining them with some political economy arguments, we have concluded that policymakers are probably well advised to stick to the conventional norm of tax neutrality, implying that the labor income of the self-employed should be taxed in roughly the same way as wage income, and that the capital income of proprietors should be taxed at roughly the same effective rate as other forms of capital income.

In Part III we argued that the so-called "Fence model" of splitting the income from self-employment is not well suited to meet this criterion of tax neutrality. Under the Fence model, income retained in the proprietor's business is taxed at a concessionary rate (e.g., at the flat corporate tax rate), and only income withdrawn from the business is taxed as ordinary personal income. It was found that such a system might create an unfortunate "locking-in" of saving as well as consumption activities in proprietorships.

In Part IV we therefore switched the attention to the "Source model" of splitting the income from self-employment. The Source model divides the income of the self-employed into an estimated income from capital, which is taxed at the flat tax rate applying to capital income, and an estimated income from labor, which is taxed progressively as earned income. This procedure raises the question whether one should start out imputing a wage income to the proprietor and treat the residual business profit as capital income, or whether one should instead impute a return to the capital invested in the firm and treat the residual business income as labor income. We argued that the latter alternative is the preferable one, partly for reasons of administrative feasibility, vertical equity, and macroeconomic stabilization, and partly because our earlier analysis of risk issues suggested an efficiency case for offering income insurance to the self-employed through progressive taxation of residual profits. We then discussed a number of practical problems involved in the imputation of a capital income to proprietors. These problems relate to the identification and valuation of business assets, to the treatment of financial assets and liabilities, and to the choice of a proper imputed rate of return including an appropriate risk premium. Our discussion of these issues indicated that policymakers may hope to achieve at best a rough measure of the "true" capital income of proprietors.

Part V then proceeded to review the actual tax rules for income from self-employment applied in the Nordic countries after the recent tax reforms. We noted that while Finland and Norway adopted pure versions of the Source model of income splitting, Denmark and Sweden introduced a rather complex hybrid between the Source model and the Fence model, offering a favorable tax treatment of residual profits retained in the business.

Clearly, our analysis has left out some important problems of taxing income from self-employment. Thus, we have focused on the problems of *splitting* the income of proprietors rather than on the problems of *measuring total income.* Moreover, a further discussion of the difficulties of identifying and valuing the "business" assets of proprietors (including intangibles) might have been warranted. We will leave these and other related problems for future research.

REFERENCES

Arnott, R. and J.E. Stiglitz (1991), "Moral Hazard and Nonmarket Institutions: Dysfunctional Crowding Out or Peer Monitoring?," *Am. Ec. Rev.*, vol. 81, pp. 179-190.

Banerjee, A. and T. Besley (1991), "Moral Hazard, Limited Liability and Taxation: A Principal-Agent Model", in Sinclair and Slater (eds.), *Taxation, Private Information and Capital*, Oxford: Clarendon Press.

De Meza, D. and D.C. Webb (1987), "Too Much Investment: A Problem of Asymmetric Information?," *Quarterly Journal of Economics*, vol. 102, pp. 281-292.

Fama, E.F. and M.C. Jensen (1983a), "Separation of Ownership and Control," *Journal of Law and Economics*, vol. 26, pp. 301-326.

Fama, E.F. and M.C. Jensen (1983b), "Agency Problems and Residual Claims," *Journal of Law and Economics*, vol. 26, pp. 327-349.

Gordon, R.H. and J.K. MacKie-Mason (1993a), "How Much Do Taxes Discourage Incorporation?," Working Paper, University of Michigan.

Gordon, R.H. and J.K. MacKie-Mason (1993b), "Tax Distortions to the Choice of Organizational Form," Working Paper, University of Michigan.

Jensen, M.C. and W.H. Meckling (1977), "Theory of the Firm: Managerial Behavior, Agency Costs and Ownership Structure," *Journal of Finance*, pp. 305-60.

Jorgenson, D.W. and K.-Y. Yun (1991), *Tax Reform and the Cost of Capital*, New York: Oxford University Press.

Keeton, W. (1979), *Equilibrium Credit Rationing*, New York: Garland Press.

King, M.A. and D. Fullerton (1984), (eds.), *The Taxation of Income From Capital*, University of Chicago Press.

Lippman, S. and J. McCall (1982), "Taxation, Incentives and Risk Sharing," *Operations Research Letters*, pp. 83-84.

Miller, M.H. (1977), "Debt and Taxes," *Journal of Finance*, vol. 32, pp. 261-75.

Mirlees, J.A. (1991), "Taxing Uncertain Incomes," in Sinclair and Slater (eds.), *Taxation, Private Information and Capital*, Oxford: Clarendon Press.

Stiglitz, J.E. and A. Weiss (1981), "Credit Rationing in Markets with Imperfect Information," *American Economic Review*, vol. 71, pp. 393-410.

Sørensen, P.B. (1994), "From the Global Income Tax to the Dual Income Tax: Recent Tax Reforms in the Nordic Countries," *Int'l Tax and Public Finance*, vol. 1, pp. 57-79.

Williamson, S.D. (1986), "Costly Monitoring, Financial Intermediation, and Equilibrium Credit Rationing," *Journal of Monetary Economics*, vol. 97, pp. 89-108.

TABLE 1. *The "gross" versus the "net" method of splitting income from selfemployment.*

INCOME STATEMENT	
Sales revenue	500,000
Business	200,000
Profits before interest ("gross" profits)	300,000
Interest on business debt (10%)	80,000
Profits net of interest ("net" profits)	220,000

BALANCE SHEET			
Assets		Liabilities	
Business Assets:	100,000	Business debt:	800,000
		Net worth:	200,000
	100,000		1,000,000

INCOME SPLITTING ACCORDING TO "GROSS" METHOD			
1.	"Gross" business assets		1,000,000
2.	Imputed return (10% of 1.)		100,000
3.	Earned income	= gross profits - imputed return = 300,000 - 100,000	200,000
4.	Capital Income	= imputed return - interest expenses = 100,000 - 80,000	20,000

INCOME SPLITTING ACCORDING TO "NET" METHOD			
1.	"Net" business assets (1,000,000 - 80,000)		200,000
2.	Imputed return (10% of 1.)		20,000
3.	Earned income	= net profits - imputed return = 220,000 - 20,000	200,000
4.	Capital income	= imputed return	20,000

APPENDIX

The Effect of a Linear Income Tax on the Trade-off Between Risk and Return

Assume that the owner has a quadratic utility function $U(x) = x - \beta x^2$, where $\beta > 0$ and $1 - 2\beta x \geq 0$. Moreover, he is ordering probability distributions for income according to the expected utility criterion, i.e.,

$$\int_x U(x)dF(x) = \mu - \beta(\sigma^2 + \mu^2)$$

where F(x) is the distribution function, μ is the mean and σ the standard deviation.

Assume there are two risky income streams with distribution functions F(s) and G(x) associated with two ownership structures. Assume further that before taxes the owner is indifferent with respect to the two. That means

$$\int_x U(x)dF(x) = \mu_F - \beta\left(\sigma_F^2 + \mu_F^2\right) = \mu_G - \beta\left(\sigma_G^2 + \mu_G^2\right) = \int_x U(x)dG(x)$$

where the subscripts refer to the respective distribution functions.

We can assume that distribution function F has the highest mean and standard deviation, i.e., $\mu_F > \mu_G$ and $\sigma_F > \sigma_G$, so that F is the more risky distribution.

Introducing a linear income tax with full loss offset yields

$$\int_x U((1-t)x)dF(x) - \int_x U((1-t)x)dG(x) = t(1-t)\beta\left[\left(\mu_F^2 + \sigma_F^2\right) - \left(\mu_G^2 + \sigma_G^2\right)\right] > 0$$

Hence, even though the owner is indifferent between the two risky income streams before taxes, he will under a linear tax prefer the more risky income after taxes. In that sense, a linear income tax would favor the ownership structure with the highest risk for the owner.

AUSTRIA'S STEPS TOWARDS A DUAL INCOME TAX

BERND GENSER

*University of Konstanz**

I. INTRODUCTION

Since January 1, 1994, Austrian capital owners who earn interest income from domestic bank deposits and bonds or who receive dividend income from domestic companies are no longer liable to the progressive income tax, but pay a final withholding tax levied at a flat rate of 22%. Compared to the top rate of 55% of the progressive income tax schedule (fig. 1), this tax reform constitutes considerable tax relief for capital owners and might be regarded as a switch to a dual income tax.

Capital income from domestic financial assets earned by companies is subject to the withholding tax as well, but for them the source tax remains a tax prepayment, which is credited against the corporation tax liability.

Although the new Austrian withholding tax regime has not been implemented under the banner "dual income taxation," it has attracted attention in other countries, where such a separation of labor and capital income taxation is a matter of discussion (cf. Sørensen 1994,

* I owe thanks to Gerald Heidiger (Graz) for informative discussions and to Andreas Haufler (Konstanz) and Ruud Okker (The Hague) for critical remarks and helpful comments on the first version of the paper.

Cnossen 1995, Mutén 1995). This paper, by describing and evaluating the final withholding tax, aims to discover whether Austria has indeed adopted a dual income tax or has at least made a major step in that direction.

The paper is organized as follows. Part II sets out the characteristic features of the long-term restructuring process of the Austrian tax system. Next, Part III concentrates on the Austrian income tax reform of 1988, and Part IV tackles the traditional problems of interest income taxation. The steps made in 1993 toward the final withholding tax are described in Part V, and the tax's legal (constitutional) foundation is summarized in Part VI. Part VIII presents a preliminary evaluation of the final withholding tax, compared to the benchmark cases of a comprehensive income tax and a perfect dual income tax. Part IX concludes with as outlook for further reform steps that should be considered in order to eliminate some inconsistencies in the prevailing tax structure, but which do not necessarily lead to a full-fledged dual income tax.

II. THE BASIC FEATURES OF THE AUSTRIAN INCOME TAX SYSTEM

Since 1945, the Austrian income tax system has been oriented towards the Schanz-Haig-Simons standard of comprehensive and progressive income taxation.[33]

Nevertheless, two important departures from the progressive and synthetic income tax system can be identified. In the early seventies, the first purely social-democratic government changed from family taxation to individual taxation and replaced traditional, personal tax allowances by personal tax credits. Both measures were based on equity arguments in favor of dual labor-income households in the lower income classes. Although a couple of counter arguments have been raised against the validity of these views,[34] the individual is still the taxable unit and

---

[33]. In 1945, the tax code of the German Reich was adopted in Austria as well as in Germany, and despite major tax reforms in both countries over the last 50 years, similarities still exist in the present tax codes that can be traced back to this common root.

[34]. The equity argument is severely eroded by the possibility of a "de facto" splitting of household income from other sources. Empirical evidence shows asset sharing by spouses in order to spread household income and to benefit from individual income taxation. The superiority of the tax credit over the tax allowance is only a formal one, as long as the tax allowance (which is equivalent to a tax reduction that increases with the marginal tax rate) is a fixed amount of money. It is always possible to compensate for the rising tax relief of the tax allowance by increasing the marginal rates of the tax scale. So it is for the German income tax, where the basic tax allowance (Grundfreibetrag) is not deducted from the tax base, but is integrated in the tax formula.

personal tax credits are still the most important tax instruments in the income tax code of 1995. A remarkable exception from comprehensive income taxation is the introduction of a separate tax schedule for the holiday and Christmas bonuses of labor-income earners. These bonuses are taxable at a preferential rate of 6% as long as they do not exceed an upper threshold of one-sixth of the annual amount of regular wages and salaries.[35] The preferential treatment of extra bonuses has led to collective wage agreements and social insurance pensions based on 14 instead of 12 monthly wage payments. The two extra monthly wages paid either semi-annually or quarterly and labor income earners are entitled to proportional shares of these extra bonuses if their job ends within the year. This tax preference for employed income must be seen as the first important deviation from comprehensive income taxation in Austria.[36]

In the 1980s the double taxation of distributed profits by the corporate income tax (CIT) and the personal income tax (PIT) was put on the tax policy agenda, since such double taxation was considered to impede the development of the Austrian capital market. A tax relief measure that mitigated the double taxation of dividends had already been granted before. Only half the regular corporate tax rate[37] had been levied on distributed profits since 1969.[38] In addition, a withholding tax of 25% was levied on cash dividends, which was credited against the personal income tax liability, whereas the reduced corporate income tax was not. Interestingly, Austria neither extended its income tax credit system to corporate income taxes nor exempted dividend payments, but rather introduced a preferential treatment of capital income from distributed profits at the personal level. The tax rate to be applied was only half the average income tax rate determined

35. In 1995 extra bonuses up to 23,000 AS are exempted under the flat-rate regime. Preferential flat rates below 6% for labor-income earners according to the number of dependent children were abolished in 1989, as well as the preferential treatment of another 8500 AS of extra bonuses in excess of two monthly wage pay-outs.

36. The flat rate schedule is also applied to compulsory severance payments based on law or on collective wage contracts. The entitlement for severance pay depends on the duration of the work contract within one enterprise and rises progressively from one month's pay after three years up to 12 months' pay after 25 years.

37. An average tax rate of 55% was levied on corporate profits exceeding a threshold income of about 1.1 million AS. For small-scale companies with lower annual profits, lower tax rates, viz. 30%, 40% and 50%, were applied.

38. The effective corporate tax rate on dividends was higher because the corporate tax liability had to be paid from retained profits, which were charged with the full corporate tax rate t. This "shadow effect" increased the preferential distribution rate $t^c/2$ according to $(t^c/2)/(1-t^c/2)$ by more than one-third in the highest rate schedule, viz. from 27.5% to 37.9%.

in the notice of annual income tax assessment. This "double semi-rate method" eliminated the double income taxation of dividends and largely leveled the playing field for the returns on investment. The tax load on retained corporate profits (55% CIT plus 0% PIT), on distributed corporate profits (37.93% CIT plus 19.24% PIT, yielding a total tax burden of 57.17%)[39] and on non-incorporated entrepreneurial profits (62% PIT) approximated each other.

Nevertheless, a couple of loopholes remained in the level playing field envisaged for the taxation of capital income. Private capital gains, for instance, were tax exempt after a holding period of one year for equities and ten years for private property, corporate profits distributed to a parent company were taxed at the reduced CIT rate, but there was no recouping tax when the profits were retained in the holding company; and, finally, interest on financial assets escaped personal income taxation to a large extent, since the tax authorities were unable to monitor the correct filing of interest income in tax returns.

Although the tax reforms of the seventies and eighties improved the Austrian tax system (judged by commonly accepted equity and efficiency standards), some loopholes in labor and capital income taxation remain, and the comprehensive income standard, although still the general principle, continued to be violated.

III. THE AUSTRIAN TAX REFORM OF 1989

The tax reform of 1989 was considered to be the first stage of a major restructuring of the Austrian tax system by the incumbent coalition government; it was influenced largely by the worldwide trend of lowering tax rates and broadening tax bases.

The top PIT was reduced from 62% to 50%. The CIT rate was reduced from 55% to 30%. In addition, the lower CIT rate was abolished and since 1989 the same rate is levied on both retained and distributed profits. Austria thereby returned to the classical corporate income tax, but the double taxation of dividends is still mitigated by the semi-rate income tax. Neutrality prevails largely for distributed profits from corporate (30% CIT plus 17.5% PIT) and non-corporate enterprises

39. Due to the shadow effect, the corporate income tax burden on distributed earnings rises to $(t^c/2)/(1-t^c/2)$, viz. 37.93% instead of 27.5% in the top bracket. The tax base of the income tax is the cash dividend; the effective income tax rate related to the dividend gross of corporate tax thus amounts to $(t^i/2)/(1+(t^c/2)/(1-t^c))$, viz. 19.24% instead of 31% in the top bracket.

(50% PIT), but the preferential treatment of retained corporate profits (30% CIT provides a strong incentive for firms to incorporate and to retain earnings. But this has been the underlying economic objective, since the government envisages a long-term improvement of the international competitiveness of Austrian firms that are organized in corporations rather than in the traditional form of proprietary businesses or partnerships.

To cope with the dramatic income tax evasion of interest income,[40] the authorities introduced a withholding tax of 10% on interest-bearing assets. Banks and financial institutions were obliged to withhold a flat tax on interest at source when interest payments to the creditor were made and the interest rate was higher than 1%. The source tax on interest income became the third pillar of withholding taxes within the Austrian income tax system, and like the other two withholding taxes (the wage tax and the dividend tax), it is also creditable against the assessed, annual income tax liability.

The rate of 10% was chosen at a much lower level than the traditional withholding tax on dividends of 25%. Three reasons have influenced that decision: First, the flat rate of 10% corresponded to the interest surtax (Zinsertragsteuer), which was introduced in 1983 but was abolished two years later due to political opposition and a decision of the Austrian Constitutional Court that the tax was unconstitutional. Second, in 1989 a 10% withholding tax on interest income took effect in Germany, which reduced the danger of cross-border capital flight. Finally, the 10% withholding tax was regarded to be sufficient with respect to budgetary needs, compensating about one-fourth of the revenue foregone through the tax reform of 1989.

The introduction of the source tax on interest proved to be a success – in particular for the federal fisc, which receives the major part of the revenue. The aggregate savings quota was hardly affected by the interest tax. For domestic financial investors no major incentive for capital flight existed, and foreign investors were exempt – although they have to certify their residency and thus give up anonymity. But foreign as well as domestic investors were convinced that the introduction of

40. The percentage of interest income declared in tax returns was estimated to be less than 10%. The income tax statistic of 1988 includes an amount of less than 4 billion AS of income from capital– compared to an estimate of roughly 100 billion AS (based on national accounts). Taking into account statistical problems in the separation of various income sources, as well as the existence of specific income tax allowances, the share of income tax evasion with respect to interest income is nevertheless estimated to be more than 80%.

the source tax was a credible guarantee for the future of the Austrian bank secrecy law, and as a result the influx of financial assets across the border even increased.

This experience was in marked contrast with Germany, where the introduction of the 10% source tax led to a short-term portfolio adjustment and had already been abolished by the end of June 1989, after half a year. Fiscal revenue from the new source tax in Austria turned out to be stable and much higher than expected between 1989 and 1992 (Table 1). Basically, the higher revenue reflects the rise in nominal interest rates. Besides this effect, which was not fully anticipated in the budget planning process, an additional portfolio allocation effect was triggered by the increasing sensitivity of domestic private investors to interest rate differentials in the face of increased competition among financial institutions.

IV THE VIOLATION OF TAX EQUITY THROUGH ANONYMITY AND BANK SECRECY

The savings quota in post-war Austria was particularly low and the population evinced little readiness to deposit money in personal savings accounts. To promote bank saving, the parliament repealed a paragraph of the general tax code (Abgabenordnung) in 1948 and permitted the opening of bank savings and deposit accounts under fictitious names or numbers without any identification. This anonymity protection has been supported and extended by the bank secrecy guarantee in the financial market law (§ 23 Kreditwesengesetz), a paragraph that became constitutional law in 1988 and can be repealed or amended only by a qualified majority of two-thirds in the Austrian parliament.

Bank secrecy in Austria is therefore of a higher quality than in most other European countries and it is nearly impossible, consequently, for the tax authorities to monitor and to control the correct payment of income taxes on interest income. As in Germany, as appeal was made to the Constitutional Court, arguing that anonymity and bank secrecy violate equality before the tax law.

In contrast to the German Constitutional Court, which argued that bank secrecy violated constitutional rights and required an efficient form of interest income taxation, the Austrian Constitutional Court rejected the view that anonymity violates constitutional rights. The decision conceded that the federal legislator may take measures to avoid capital flight or to protect privacy, even if these measures create problems in the administration and control of tax laws. Even if tax loopholes are used for tax evasion and equity norms of taxation are infringed upon, this does not render tax laws unconstitutional. The Court took as given that the tax authority tries its best to detect tax evasion and that offenders are fined sufficiently to deter evasion.

The Court's decision confirmed that the declaration principle, viz. the reliance on individual filing of interest income, is in line with the constitution although the verification principle, viz. the efficient control of interest income filing, is severely eroded. The decision did not compel the government to modify the prevailing Austrian income tax code, in particular the principles of self-assessment and of synthetic income taxation.

It is noteworthy that the decision of the German Constitutional Court, issued in June 1991 on the nearly identical issue, was the opposite. The German Court called for a new regulation of interest taxation in Germany within 18 months, based on its view that (i) equality before the tax law must be attained in reality as well, (ii) the declaration principle of individual filing has to be complemented by the verification principle through effective control and (iii) even economic objectives of national importance do not overrule the obligation for sufficient control of tax equity.

A second question concerns an apparent economic inconsistency between two decisions of the Austrian Court on interest taxation. The revealed conformity of unenforceable Austrian interest taxation with constitutional equity norms, stated in 1991, contrasts with the ban of the 10% interest surtax, which was levied as a source tax between 1983 and 1985. This surtax was declared unconstitutional, since it was not credited against the income tax liability and therefore created a light double taxation burden for honest tax compliers.

Although the Austrian government was not forced to enact an income tax reform like the German one, equity problems and revenue losses were nevertheless regarded to be serious and political discussions paved the way to the introduction of the final tax on interest income.

Two arguments were important: First, income and wealth taxes are levied on the nominal values of interest income and principal, and the combined imposition of these taxes is likely to turn the net real return on financial assets negative. Even the rather favorable nominal interest rate of 8% in the late 1980s gave rise to a real loss of the principal for the honest taxpayer due to the combined tax burden of the income tax (50%) and the wealth tax (1%), when the inflation rate exceeded 3%. The danger of real loss in financial assets is exacerbated when increasing interest rates reduce the price of a loan, but income and wealth taxes take no account of this change in wealth. A negative real return or a loss in wealth induced by the tax system is regarded as a violation of the constitutional right of property protection.

Second, interest-bearing assets are discriminated against compared to returns on other forms of wealth, physical or human capital, for which the Austrian tax code provides shelters against inflation. The distortionary effects of inflation are caused by the fiscal drag of a progressive income tax, which increases the tax burden even if nominal income growth compensates only for rising prices. Further distortions are produced by fictitious profits due to the inadequate valuation of depreciation costs or inventories based on historical prices or by the strategic postponement of income tax payments. Tax shelters against inflationary losses comprise investment tax credits, accelerated depreciation, tax-free reserves for enterprises and the self-employed, employee tax credits, labor-related allowances, the flat rate taxation of holiday and Christmas bonuses, preferential presumptive taxes on farm and forestry income and the preferential taxation of capital gains. The only source of income that is fully exposed to inflationary erosion is interest income, since nominal interest is taxed, irrespective of whether the interest compensates for losses of the principal or generated gains in real wealth.

V. THE MOVE TO THE FINAL WITHHOLDING TAX IN 1993

Once more parallel to Germany, Austria modified its source tax on interest income in 1993. In Germany, the new 30% withholding tax on interest income (Zinsabschlagsteuer) is credited against the personal income tax liability. At the same time, the personal interest income allowance was raised by a factor 10 to 6000 DM per capita per year. In order to avoid tax rebates for the majority of citizens with interest income below the threshold, authorities allow taxpayers an exemption from the withholding tax for their interest income below the personal allowance level. Special exemption forms can be submitted to the financial institutions, which pay out gross interest without a withholding tax as long as interest payments are below the individually specified exemption level. Exemption forms are subject to control by the tax authorities, since the personal exemption allowance will generally be split among different financial institutions, and banks cannot monitor an excessive application for exemption. Due to the generous level of the interest income allowance, about 80% of the German citizens earn their interest income tax-free, and they do not have to file a tax return. Nevertheless, the administrative burden of the exemption procedure was heavily criticized as complicated and costly.

Since 1990, an expert committee[41] has had an ongoing discussion about the future of interest taxation within Austria. When the German solution became known, the Austrian government decided to implement the new system of interest taxation in 1993, one year before the announced second stage of the tax reform of the still-incumbent coalition cabinet.

The basic feature of the interest tax reform of 1993 was the move to a final withholding tax on interest income. The withholding tax rate of 22% became the final tax for interest income that domestic savers earned on private financial wealth held in domestic banks. The final tax covered not only the income tax liability, but also the wealth tax and the inheritance tax. The tax base of the final tax is the amount of gross interest payments. Costs of earning interest income cannot be deducted, and no basic exemption exists for low-income earners. Low-income earners are, however, offered an assessment option for their gross interest income via their annual tax return, and they will receive a tax rebate if the prepaid withholding tax exceeds the personal income tax liability. Foreigners, which are not subject to unrestricted income taxation in Austria, are exempted from the withholding tax upon personal application and declaration of their residency status.

Interest income on financial assets held in the business sphere continues to be taxable under the PIT or the CIT, and the tax withheld on interest income is creditable. An assessment regulation was also

---

41. This expert group is a working group of the "Tax Reform Commission," which was installed as early as 1979. Whereas the large Commission was mainly a discussion forum (especially in the first years), the working group on business taxation, headed by Gerald Heidinger, became influential and took the lead in sketching the guidelines for the majority of reform steps in the last 15 years.

chosen for those private financial assets that are used as collateral for business debt.

From an economic point of view, the final withholding tax on interest income aims at three primary targets: (i) The withholding tax covers all interest income and stops the discrimination against honest taxpayers. Equity among interest earners is reestablished – in the sense that all of them pay an income tax on interest, and tax evasion is reduced to returns from financial assets, which are not taxed at source (e.g. interest from foreign banks or from private debtors). (ii) The final tax rate of 22% is less than half of the maximum income tax rate on other forms of taxable income (Fig. 1). If we assume that half of the interest income is compensation for the inflationary erosion of the principal, then the lower withholding tax on total interest is by and large equivalent to an exemption of the inflation element. This re-establishes the equal treatment of interest income with other sources of income that are not taxed on inflationary gains (capital gains of equity shares or private property) or those that enjoy tax preferences to mitigate the effects of over-valued, nominal tax bases. (iii) The final withholding tax on gross interest income is a cheap and efficient way of collecting taxes.

VI. THE LEGAL FOUNDATION OF THE FINAL WITHHOLDING TAX

The final withholding tax on interest income was introduced by means of a constitutional law, the Endbesteuerungsgesetz (BGB1. 11/1993), and of amendments of various related tax laws – the income tax law, the wealth tax law, the inheritance and gift tax law, the valuation law, etc..

The decision of the government and the parliament to back the tax reform by a constitutional law was regarded as indispensable for two reasons: (i) A final withholding tax at a preferential rate of 22% was regarded to be a break with the general principle of synthetic income taxation. Furthermore, the final tax option was offered only to private holders of interest-bearing assets, whereas interest on financial assets in the business sphere was excluded from this favorable tax treatment. This discriminatory feature of the final withholding tax would certainly have led to complaints against the tax law on the ground that it violated fundamental equity rules granted in the constitution. These reactions were avoided by passing a constitutional law. (ii) The introduction of the final withholding tax was accompanied by as general tax amnesty for the large number of cases of interest tax evasion before 1993, apart from cases already under investigation. An amnesty, of course, may also be regarded as a source of inequity, discriminating against honest taxpayers.

The constitutional law comprises eight paragraphs that compel the legislator (the federal parliament) to do the following:

- to introduce by 1993 the final withholding tax, which substitutes for income taxation, wealth taxation and inheritance taxation (§1(1) and (2)),
- to define one single withholding tax rate within the narrow band of 20% and half the prevailing maximum income tax rate (§1(4)), viz. 25% at the moment,
- to provide an assessment option with a rebate of the withholding tax (§1(5)),
- to exclude the deductibility of any costs associated with interest income (§2) and
- to restrict the applicability of preferential final taxation to interest income subject to the withholding tax (§3)

In addition, the constitutional law entitles the legislator to do the following:

- to restrict the final tax to private assets that are not used as collateral for business debt (§1(3)) and
- to extend the final tax to income and wealth liabilities according to open distributions of corporate profits (§1(6)).

The remaining paragraphs force the administrative and judicial bodies to do the following:

- to grant a tax amnesty for violations of tax laws in connection with interest bearing assets, if the withholding tax is paid in 1993 (§4,5),
- to enact a special regulation for 1992 (§6) and
- to extend the amnesty to potential violations of the foreign exchange law (§7).

The legislative foundation of the final withholding tax in a constitutional law was heavily criticized by legal experts (cf. Gassner, 1993, 8ff). They emphasize that the constitutional law strictly limits the control of the final tax by the Constitutional Court. In particular, potential violations of equity norms as well as the guarantee of property norms caused by the final tax can no longer be scrutinized and disclosed because most of the tax rules have become part of the Constitution.

Prominent experts of public law (Gassner 1993, 11) assert that the final tax could have been introduced as a simple tax law, without constitutional backing as well, in line with past decisions of the Court. Experts also complained that there had been no official appraisal procedure of the government bill, both in public and among experts, which would have allowed discussion of the legal problems of the final withholding tax proposal.

VII. THE EXTENSION OF THE FINAL WITHHOLDING TAX WITHIN THE TAX REFORM OF 1994

The main objective of the Austrian tax reform of 1994 was a relief in business taxation to secure the international competitiveness of Austria in the European internal market. The most important signals sent by the tax reform are the abolition of the business tax[42] and the abolition of the wealth tax.[43] The tax relief offered by these measures was compensated partly by the rise of the CIT rate to 34% (compared to 30% before) and by the reduction of a number of traditional tax preferences.[44]

With respect to the final withholding tax, three extensions were implemented. (i) The "business security proviso," which excludes interest on private financial assets used to secure business debt, was abolished retroactively from January 1993, and thus never became effective. (ii) The final withholding tax was extended to interest income of non-incorporated enterprises. In the amendment to the constitutional

42. The business tax on business assets, under discussion in Germany at the moment, had already been abolished in three steps between 1984 and 1986; a reduction of the tax rate and tax preferences for small-scale businesses were elements of the tax reform of 1989 (See Genser/Holzmann 1993).

43. The Austrian wealth tax was raised on personal as well as corporate assets and thus gave rise to a double taxation of the capital stock of corporations. A first relief of double taxation was offered in 1989, when the wealth tax of corporations was acknowledged as deductible from the corporate income tax base. A second tax burden on corporate wealth, the "Inheritance Tax Equivalent" (Erbschaftsteueräquivalent), was also abolished.

44. The tax-free-investment reserve was abolished and the investment allowance reduced to 15% (and finally to 9% in 1995). A minimum CIT was also introduced.

final tax law (§1(3)), the legislator is obliged to exempt interest income in the business sphere from the assessed income-tax base; the withholding tax on gross interest payments is thus final. But the final tax for businesses does not include the inheritance tax. (iii) The most important extension is the final taxation of distributed profits from equity shares of domestic companies (§1(1)). Again the final tax replaces only the PIT liability and not the inheritance tax liability.

Two general principles of the first-round final tax version carry over to the second-round extension. First, the option for income-tax assessment remains and in these cases the withheld tax is credited against the PIT liability. Second, gross capital income is the relevant tax base for the withholding tax as well as for filed income. It is not possible to deduct business expenses related to the purchase of financial assets. The break with the principle of net income reduces, of course, the attractiveness of the filing option and is likely to render superfluous the preferential taxation of income from distributed profits introduced in 1989.

VIII. A FIRST ECONOMIC EVALUATION OF THE AUSTRIAN DUAL INCOME TAX

The extension of final withholding taxation to interest and dividend income flowing to non-incorporated businesses gives the impression of a rather generous treatment of capital income in Austria. This shift towards a dual income tax is certainly the reason why the Austrian tax reform has received attention in the academic world, but as such this shift would certainly not suffice to explain the remarkably positive echo from tax practitioners and the broad political support in the Austrian parliament.

Two evident attractive features of the Austrian final withholding tax are the low costs of its administration and its contribution to distributional equity.

Whereas the cost argument is certainly true for the collection of the withholding tax, it is questionable for the filing option. Compliance costs may not be larger for taxpayers, who have to file anyway. For them there is just an additional comparison between the final tax option and the filing option ex-post. But there will be considerable compliance costs for taxpayers who gain from filing due to low income. On the other hand, the number of taxpayers opting for filing is expected to be low.

Distributional equity has two facets which work in opposite directions. Since only a small part of interest income had been reported in the past (due to anonymity and bank secrecy), a positive contribution to equity by taxing a huge amount of evaded income at source can hardly be denied. The imposition of a final tax on interest income at 22% which would otherwise have been taxed at 10% when not filed, certainly reduces the inequality of after-tax incomes. On the other hand, the 22% final tax is, after all, a remarkable tax relief to those high income earners who did not want or were not able to evade taxes on capital income in the past and who will face an increase of their after-tax income.

The tax relief argument, which rests on the low final rate of 22%, also needs some economic qualification. From a comprehensive income perspective, the change in real wealth is the relevant indicator of ability-to-pay, and interest income would be judged to be overtaxed if inflationary losses of financial assets are not accounted for. If overtaxation is regarded as a discriminatory flaw of the prevailing income tax system and the comparison is based on an income tax system that taxes real interest income, then the tax relief shrinks to the difference between the regular tax rate on real interest income and the hypothetical tax rate on real interest income, which is equivalent to the low withholding tax rate on nominal interest income. With i and r being the nominal and the real interest rate, respectively, and p the inflation rate, we get for the hypothetical tax rate t^h

$$t^h r = 0.22i = 0.22(r+p) = 0.22(r+\beta i) = (0.22/(1-\beta))r$$

where β is the inflation component of nominal interest, viz. $p = \beta i$. For β between 30% and 60%, we get t^h between 30% and 55%. Tax relief will presumably turn out for only top-decile income earners, who face a low β, given the fact that they earn a higher nominal interest rate on their assets. In this income group the hypothetical rate might therefore be smaller than the regular marginal income tax rate of 50%, the top rate of the Austrian income tax schedule.

The tax relief due to final taxation of distributed profits must be measured in terms of the semi-tax rate for dividends at the personal level. The cumulative tax rate T^c from corporate and final withholding taxes on a gross dividend of one, therefore, is

$$T^c = 0.34 + 0.22(1\text{-}0.34) = 0.4852$$

Compared to the semi-rate income taxation of 1993 (and a CIT tax of 30%), the tax burden under the final withholding tax corresponds to an average income tax rate $T^h = 0.5291$, given implicitly by

$$T^c = 0{,}4852 = 0.3 + (T^h/2)(1\text{-}0.3)$$

which is higher than the top PIT rate of 50%. Thus, apart from the tax relief generated by the abolition of the wealth and the business tax, no further net income gain can be expected through the final withholding taxation of dividends.

Interest income that does not qualify for the final withholding tax must still be taxed according to the regular income schedule. This is true for interest income from private loans or from foreign assets. These forms of interest income will remain overtaxed (and thus discriminated against if they are reported).

The preferential treatment of capital income raises the question whether there exist possibilities to transform income from regularly taxed sources into capital income subject to the flat-rate final tax. While it is true that strategic tax arbitrage is of primary importance in a full-fledged, dual income-tax system, when problems of monitoring and controlling tax avoidance through the transformation of labor income into lowly taxed capital income are well known, the Austrian withholding tax does not offer such arbitrage opportunities on a noteworthy scale. The withholding tax on distributed profits offers only a negligibly low arbitrage gain of less than 2% (see above), and so it hardly pays to swap labor income for dividend income. Swapping labor income for interest income does not pay either, since private interest income from non-banks is not subject to the final withholding tax and no promising way seems to exist to re-channel factor income via interest payments through banks or investment funds.

The final withholding tax, however, does not close tax loopholes created by tax preferences offered to financial intermediaries such as pension funds or non-profit foundations. If these institutions qualify for CIT exemption, no withholding tax is levied on the interest income that they earn on their financial assets. The preferential treatment of certain forms of contractual savings via pension claims, life insurance claims, as well as private capital gains is not touched by the final withholding tax and thus remains unresolved.

Another general problem introduced by final withholding taxation is the break with the net income principle (Beiser 1994, 150 ff.). While broad agreement exists that source taxation should be based on gross income, and this fact is also the justification for using the low withholding rate, the final withholding tax law states that the gross income principle must also be applied if the filing option is chosen. It is clear that final withholding taxation of capital income can lead to much higher tax burdens once the deductibility of business expenses, e.g. debt services, is excluded. Since the main objective of the introduction of the withholding tax was to reduce tax evasion, no economic justification can be found for levying an additional tax burden on capital income. Although the Austrian income tax code already contains a number of limitations on the deductibility of business expenses (e.g. business meals, business cars), the non-deductibility of costs for business credit creates a new and disturbing departure from the net income principle. A distortion of financing decisions, given their importance and sensitivity in business policy, may generate high costs, and authorities should consider complementing the filing option by a deductibility of business expenses.

A final problem needing further discussion (cf. Beiser, 1994) is the interaction of the withholding tax on dividends and the capital gains tax upon sales of assets. If shares are sold before the annual dividends are paid out, then distributed profits will be double-taxed. They are included in the equity price and taxed (at a reduced rate) as capital gains upon sale. They will be taxed again, when the withholding tax is levied on the dividends. This form of double taxation does not occur for securities, because the interest payment is known in advance and can be precisely attributed to the seller and the buyer, whenever the purchase takes place. The solution for equity sales might thus be a deduction of anticipated dividends or an equivalent tax concession, whereas no change is required for the final withholding tax. Yet, we must stress that this is no new problem generated by the final withholding tax.

IX. TAX REFORM PERSPECTIVES FOR THE AUSTRIAN FINAL WITHHOLDING TAX

Critical remarks on the existing final withholding tax regime raise the question whether further scope exists for improving the dual income tax.

First, a series of legal problems exist, which should be taken seriously. In particular, the passing of a tax bill as a constitutional law must be regarded as an alarming precedent and any attempt to continue such a policy must be avoided. Although specific constitutional amendments have some tradition in the Austrian parliamentary history, the elections of October 1994 might have changed the situation, since the two large parties lost their qualified (two thirds) majority in the Austrian parliament for the first time since 1945 and constitutional laws require political support by members of one of the three other parties.

A further extension of final withholding taxes does not seem very promising as long as the tax authorities cannot efficiently control these source taxes. But proposals to avoid discriminatory taxation of assessed interest income should be considered, e.g., the application of the semi-rate to nominal interest income. This solution would not only end allocative distortions in the capital market, it would also be in line with the distributional target of reducing the tax burden for low income earners by assessment.

Another discriminatory element from a distributional perspective is the inheritance tax component included in the final withholding tax on interest payments to non-business persons but not on other capital income or business interest income. Although it can be argued that the creation of different degrees of final taxation is undesirable, I doubt that there will be a gain in equity if the final flat-rate tax would cover the inheritance tax generally. Discussion in Austria about the future of the inheritance tax (cf. Heidinger, 1994b)is ongoing. However, since we have it now, a preferential treatment of financial assets seems justified as long as real property is greatly undervalued[45] in the inheritance and gift tax base.

An amendment to the final withholding tax law would be necessary to reintroduce the net-income principle for capital income that is declared in the income tax return. Trading off the economic costs

---

45. Unit values (Einheitswerte), which reflect only a small fraction of market values of real property, are the tax base for the property tax and the property acquisition tax as well.

of tax collection and potential distortions of business financing, it might be preferable to offer the possibility of net-income filing only to businesses, which have to report their business income anyway. This would of course discriminate against capital income in the private sphere, where no such deductibility is allowed. But in quantitative terms, the final withholding tax might be regarded as the most attractive taxation method in general. If a large number of private individuals would be better off by filing their net capital income, then lowering the withholding tax rate level is likely to be the preferred policy response.

Although the changeover to a flat-rate capital income tax is widely regarded to be a farewell to the traditional equity standard and the ability-to-pay principle of modern income taxation, I do not think that this view does justice to the recent Austrian tax reforms. I would rather appraise the measures in terms of a response to equity loopholes of income taxation in economic reality, in line with second-best tax rules if income cannot be efficiently monitored by the tax authorities. I think that future tax reforms will have to pay more attention to other deviations from the pure synthetic income tax standard and that further elements of presumptive taxation might offer a welfare-improving solution to tax policy problems.

REFERENCES

Beiser, Reinhold (1993) "Beteiligungsveräußerungen und Endbesteuerung–Gedanken und Vorschläge zur Steuerreform 1993."*Österreichische Steuer-Zeitung* 46,279-282.

Beiser, Reinhold (1994a) "Die erweiterte Endbesteuerung." *Österreichische Steuer-Zeitung* 47, 145-154.

Beiser, Reinhold (1994a) "Reformvorschläge zur Endbesteuerung und zur Besteuerung von Beteiligungen." *Österreichische Steuer-Zeitung* 47, 327-330.

Cnossen, Sijbren (1995) "Towards a New Tax Covenant," *De Economist* 143, 1-31.

Genser, Bernd and Robert Holzmann (1993) "Die finanzpolitische Entwicklung in Österreich 1989-1990." *Finanzarchiv* 50, 94-123.

Genser, Bernd and Robert Holzmann (1995) "Die österreichische Finanzpolitik vor dem EU-Beitritt." *Forschungsbericht* 9501, Ludwig Boltzmann Institut, Vienna.

Heidinger, Gerald (1992a) "Ist die Überbesteuerung der Zinsen verfassungskonform?"*Österreichische Steuer-Zeitung* 45, 17-20.

Heidinger, Gerald (1992b) "Ist die Vermögensteuer noch zeitgemäß?" *Österreichische Steuer-Zeitung* 45, 296-301.

Heidinger, Gerald (1992c) "Steuerreform in Österreich: Halbsatzverfahren und Abgeltungssteuer." *Deutsche Steuer-Zeitung* 80, 456-459.

Heidinger, Gerald (1993a) "Zinsenbesteuerung in Österreich. 22% Abgeltungssteuer ab 1. Januar 1993." *Deutsche Steuer-Zeitung* 81, 137-141.

Heidinger, Gerald (1993b) "Österreich - Ende der Kumulativbesteuerung am 31. Dezember 1993." *Deutsche Steuer-Zeitung* 81, 742-746.

Heidinger, Gerald (1994a) "Die erweiterte Endbesteuerung. Zur Kritik Beisers in der ÖStZ 1994/6." *Österreichische Steuer-Zeitung* 47, 263-264.

Heidinger,Gerald (1994b)"Erbschaftsteuer: Reform oder Aufhebung?"*Ecolex*, 496-501.

Heidinger, Gerald (1995) "Reformen der Unternehmens- und Kapitalbesteuerung in Österreich." *Deutsche Steuer-Zeitung* 83, 65-71.

Lang, Michael and Martin Jann (1995) "Entwicklungstendenzen in der Zinsenbesteuerung." *Internationales Steuerrecht* 2, 55-62.

Mutén, Leif (1995) "Dual Income Tax: the Scandinavian Experience." This brochure.

Quantschnigg, Peter (1994) "Erlaßregelungen zur Endbesteuerung." *Österreichische Steuer-Zeitung* 47, 205-220.

Sørensen, Peter (1994) "From the Global Income Tax to the Dual Income Tax: Recent Tax Reforms in the Nordic Countries." *International Tax and Public Finance* 1, 57-79.

TABLE 1: TAX REVENUE[a] (IN BILLIONS OF AS)

Year	Source Tax on Interest		Assessed Income Tax		Total Taxes on Income and Wealth	
1983	-		23.2		124.3	
1984	0.4		24.9		135.5	
1985	3.4		26.0		151.4	
1986	2.9		25.6		159.6	
1987	1.3		25.5		155.9	
1988	-		27.1		170.8	
1989	3.3	(3.5)	31.3		169.5	
1990	7.2	(4.5)	33.8		194.5	
1991	9.6	(7.8)	35.8		220.2	
1992	11.4	(8.8)	37.0		244.4	
1993	16.6	(20.0)	32.7		245.9	
1994	19.7	(23.0)	31.6		238.0	
1995		(21.5)		(28.0)		(239.7)

[a] Figures in brackets refer to the budget plan (Bundesvoranschlag)

Source: Amts(Arbeits-)behelf zum Bundesfinanzgesetz. Vienna, various years.

Fig. 1: Marginal income tax rate (MIT) and final withholding tax rate (FWT)

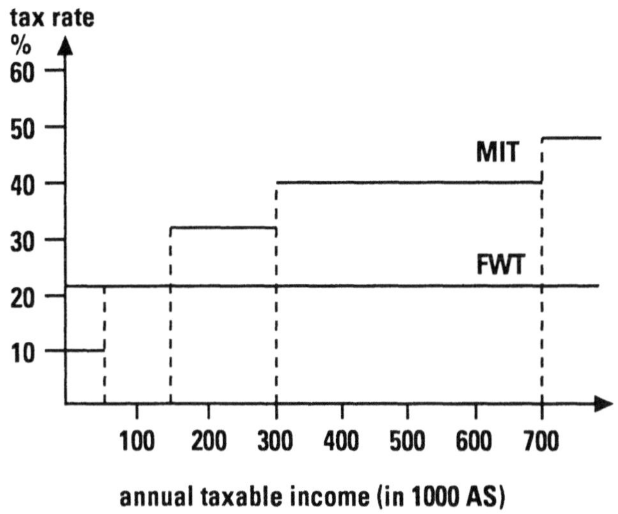

www.ingramcontent.com/pod-product-compliance
Lightning Source LLC
LaVergne TN
LVHW021114300926
849160LV00009B/731

* 9 7 8 9 0 4 1 1 0 9 2 8 6 *